DATE DUE		

HESSELBEIN

— ON —

LEADERSHIP

HESSELBEIN

— ON —

LEADERSHIP

FRANCES HESSELBEIN
FOREWORD BY JIM COLLINS

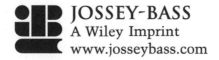

JOSSEY-BASS
A Wiley Imprint
www.josseybass.com

Published by Jossey-Bass
A Wiley Imprint
989 Market Street, San Francisco, CA 94103-1741   www.josseybass.com

Jossey-Bass books and products are available through most bookstores. To contact Jossey-Bass directly call our Customer Care Department within the U.S. at 800-956-7739, outside the U.S. at 317-572-3986, or fax 317-572-4002.

Jossey-Bass also publishes its books in a variety of electronic formats. Some content that appears in print may not be available in electronic books.

The essays in this book are drawn from issues of the Drucker Foundation's journal *Leader to Leader*, except for Chapter 1, which is from the book *The Leader of the Future*, and Chapter 2, which is from the book *The Community of the Future*. Original dates of publication are given at the end of each chapter. They are reprinted with the permission of the Peter F. Drucker Foundation for Nonprofit Management, www.drucker.org.

Library of Congress Cataloging-in-Publication Data

Hesselbein, Frances.
     Hesselbein on leadership / Frances Hesselbein; foreword by Jim Collins.
        p. cm.
Includes index.
     ISBN 0-7879-6392-5 (alk. paper)
     1. Leadership. 2. Organizational change. 3. Management. I. Title.
     HD57.7 .H47 2002
     658.4'092—dc21

                                                                                          2002009141

Printed in the United States of America

FIRST EDITION

HB Printing   10 9 8 7 6 5 4 3 2 1

This collection is dedicated to leaders everywhere who find that in the end, leadership is the great adventure.

The essays in this book are a collection from issues of the Drucker Foundation's award-winning journal *Leader to Leader* and the books *The Leader of the Future* and *The Community of the Future*. I would like to express my gratitude to my friends and colleagues of the Drucker Foundation, Jossey-Bass, and John Wiley & Sons, Inc.

CONTENTS

FOREWORD

HARRY TRUMAN once defined leadership as the art of getting people to do what they might not otherwise do, and to like it.

That quotation comes to mind whenever I get a call from Frances Hesselbein. The phone rings, I pick up, and I hear Frances on the other end of the line. "Jim, I was hoping that you might consider . . ." Or, "The foundation would so value . . ." Or, "It would be wonderful if you would think about . . ." And before I even hear the end of the sentence, I know that I will very likely say yes. I also know that I'm going to like it.

I'm not the only person who has this experience. A few years ago, I had the opportunity to present at the Drucker

Foundation annual conference, held in Los Angeles. The evening before the main event, I attended a reception. As I moved around the room full of remarkable people—thinkers, authors, corporate executives, directors of nonprofits, government leaders—I asked, "What brings you here?" The answers invariably circled back to Frances Hesselbein. Later, at the reception dinner, Peter Drucker quipped that he made a practice of doing pretty much whatever Frances asks. Like Drucker, nearly all those in the room had reached a point of being masters of their own lives. Yet when Frances calls, they all have a great propensity to say yes, and to like it.

In this delightful collection of essays, Hesselbein shares her own perspectives on the art of leadership. Like many highly effective leaders, she has so much to teach us from her own example, but she is reticent to talk much about herself—a trait you will notice in these pages. So, allow me to paint a picture of her achievements, to set the context for what you will read in this book. She is a person of substantial accomplishment from whom we can all learn, all the more so because she would never say so herself.

In 1976, Hesselbein found herself at the center of an organization cascading toward irrelevance. I'm careful here not to say "atop" the organization, as Frances would never think of her role that way. When describing her organization structure to a *New York Times* reporter, she put a glass at the center of a lunch table and created a set of concentric circles radiating outward—plates, cups, saucers—connected by knives, forks, and spoons. "I'm here," she said, pointing to the glass in the middle. "I'm not on top of anything."

But however you think of the structure, Hesselbein became CEO of the Girl Scouts of the USA at the most perilous time in its then sixty-four-year history. As John Byrne described in a *BusinessWeek* feature (from which I have drawn extensively for this foreword), Hesselbein faced challenges at least as difficult as those faced by CEOs of decaying old-line corporations: declining market share, dissatisfied customers, economic weakness, and even hostile takeover threats. "Lurking in the background like a corporate raider," wrote Byrne, "was the Boy Scouts of America [which] had launched a feasibility study of extending its membership to girls."

With eight straight years of declining membership, the Girl Scouts were in danger of going the way of the Howard Johnson motor restaurants—a classic American icon of a bygone age, increasingly passed by as people's needs and tastes changed. The Girl Scouts organization of 1976 was predominately white yet eager to serve all girls. The girls of America were fast becoming aware of their diversity, their talents, and their ambitions. They worried less about preparing for marriage and more about preparing for college and work, less about household skills and more about how to respond to increasing peer pressure to have sex or take drugs. They wanted—needed—a highly contemporary organization that could help them become leaders in the world and responsible for their own lives.

Hesselbein came into her responsibility as a consummate insider. With twenty-five years of experience, first as a volunteer troop leader and later as a local council executive director and national board member, she disproves the myth that change leaders must be larger-than-life heroes who ride in from the outside on a white horse. Dyed in green (the color of the Girl Scouts), Hesselbein vowed to defend the timeless core values of the Girl Scouts and recommitted the organization to its enduring mission of helping girls reach their highest potential. Beyond that, however, everything else would be open for change.

And change she wrought. Hesselbein believed that any girl in America—be she low-income or wealthy, urban or rural, black, white, Latina, or whatever—should be able to picture herself in the Girl Scouts. "If I'm a Navajo child on a reservation, a newly arrived Vietnamese child, or a young girl in rural Appalachia, I have to be able to open [the Girl Scout handbook] and find myself there," she said. "That's a very powerful message that 'I'm not an outsider. I'm part of something big.'" The Girl Scouts not only changed materials like the Girl Scout handbooks (even translating them into multiple languages) but also initiated a slew of new offerings. Proficiency badges sprouted up in topics like math, technology, and computer science, to reinforce the fact that girls are—and should think of themselves as—smart, capable individuals. The organization artfully moved people to confront the brutal facts facing girls in modern America, such as teen pregnancy and alcohol use among minors, by creating materials on sensitive issues. The parent organization did not force these materials down people's throats, but simply gave the interdependent councils the opportunity to use the materials at their discretion. Most did.

Hesselbein grasped a central paradox of change: the organizations that best adapt to a changing world first and foremost know what should *not* change. They have a fixed anchor of guiding principles around which they can more easily change everything else. They know the difference between what is truly sacred and what is not, between what should never change and what should be always open for change, between "what we stand for" and "how we do things." Had she marched in with a big "change program," full of herself as the great change leader, her efforts likely would have failed. Instead, she began with a rededication to the guiding values and enduring mission of the Girl Scouts as the framework for change, giving people an anchor point of stability. Yes, there would be change, but it would all be done in the spirit of reinvigorating the soul of the institution, not destroying it.

Equally important, she exercised the discipline to say no to changes and opportunities that did not fit the central mission. When a charity organization sought to partner with the Girl Scouts, envisioning an army of smiling girls going door to door to canvass for the greater good, Hesselbein commended the desire to make a difference, but gave a polite and firm no.

Hesselbein understood that to "do good" does not mean doing *all* good. To deliver the best results—and, as she continually reminds us in these essays, it is imperative to think in terms of results—requires the discipline to focus only on those activities that meet three basic tests. First, the opportunity must fit squarely in the middle of the mission. Second, the enterprise must have the capability to execute on the opportunity better than any other organization. (If not, then leave the opportunity to others.) And third, the opportunity must make sense within the context of the economic engine and resources of the institution. Hesselbein pounded out a simple mantra: "We are here for only one reason: to help a girl reach her highest potential." She steadfastly steered the Girl Scouts into those activities—and only those activities—where it could make a unique and significant contribution of value to its members. And throughout, she bolstered the financial health of the Girl Scouts, mindful of Peter Drucker's adage that the foundation for doing good is doing well.

And, indeed, the results came. Not just financial—for that is not the point in a mission-driven enterprise—but equally in terms of membership, volunteer dedication, and the enduring impact on the lives of girls. Under her leadership, the Girl Scouts regained its preeminent position, with a girl membership of 2.25 million and a workforce (mainly volunteers) of 780,000. Equally important, the organization had attained greater diversity *and* cohesion than at any time in its history—

each side of the coin reinforcing the other, in a powerful yin and yang combination. Finally, she set up the organization to be successful long into the future, beyond her tenure. Today, in 2002, the Girl Scouts of the USA has grown to nearly four million members, including nearly one million adult member volunteers.

When I think of what makes the Girl Scouts and, later, the Drucker Foundation tick at their best, I think first of the people that freely give of themselves to the mission of each organization. The theme of relationships runs as a common thread through nearly every page of these essays. For in the end, commitment to mission ultimately means commitment to other people who share the mission with you. To fail the mission is one thing, to fail other people is entirely another. And it is this magical combination of the right people engaged in common cause that Frances orchestrates as well as anyone—a fact that is borne out in her remarkable record of results.

Which brings me to the final and most important point about *Hesselbein on Leadership*. Like all of the very best executives, her ambition is first and foremost for the organization, the cause, the work—not herself. This is the central reason why she is able to get so many people to do what they might not otherwise do, and to like it. After all, in a world where the very best people are ultimately volunteers, why on earth should they give over their creative energies to advance the greater glory of a leader whose ambition is first and foremost self-centric? They shouldn't, and they don't.

Early in this book, Frances tells the story of a young person who approaches her after a presentation to ask, "Why should I not be cynical?" The answer to that question comes in Hesselbein's cardinal rule: leadership is much less about what you *do,* and much more about who you *are.* If you view leadership as a bag of manipulative tricks or charismatic behaviors to advance your own personal interests, then people have every right to be cynical. But if your leadership flows first and foremost from inner character and integrity of ambition, then you can justly ask people to lend themselves to your organization and its mission. As one of those rare individuals who displays consistency between her teachings and her own practice, there is perhaps no better answer to the question "Why should I not be cynical?" than the example of Frances Hesselbein herself.

June 2002

Jim Collins
Boulder, Colorado

HESSELBEIN
—— ON ——
LEADERSHIP

NOTE TO THE READER

THIS IS a small book for leaders who, with each challenge, define and redefine leadership in their own terms, their own language, their own behavior, performance, and results.

Whether we have been leading a team, a large corporation, a small organization, a university, or the U.S. Army, this is a time of testing; and whether we have been leading for five or twenty-five years, today's challenges demand an examination of our basic leadership definitions, values, principles, and assumptions.

This is a time of testing.

PART I

Leadership— A Matter of How to Be, Not How to Do It

HOW DO WE MOVE from where we are to where we are called to be? It all begins with the leaders' challenge to define leadership in our own terms, in our own language.

Long ago, before the Drucker Foundation, when I was CEO of the Girl Scouts of the USA, I knew I had to define leadership on my own terms and in my own language, in ways that would define who I was, why I did what I did, that would communicate and embody the heart, the spirit of the leadership I was called to provide. After long, difficult introspection, I developed my own definition of leadership: *leadership is a matter of how to be, not how to do it.*

When I was with the Girl Scouts then, and later with the Drucker Foundation, or speaking to the U.S. Army, the U.S. Coast Guard, Chevron, Texaco, the World Bank, Hewlett-Packard, Vice President Gore's Reinventing Government Conference, Head Start, Evangelical Lutheran Women's Conference, Bright China Management Institute, and many colleges and universities, this was and is my definition of leadership. It defines who I am, why I do what I do, what I believe. I test it over and over. And in the end, I know that it is the quality and character of the leader that determines the performance, the results.

All the how to's in the world won't work until the "how to be's" are defined, embraced by the leaders, and embodied and demonstrated in every action, every communication, every leadership moment. Leaders at every level in every enterprise can disperse the tasks of leadership across the organization, until we have not a leader, but leaders of character at every level, leading the organization and the community of the future.

After September 11, 2001, I reread the essays in this book, and I found that my personal definition of leadership still holds. In the weeks after the country lost over 3,000 of its people in deadly terrorist attacks, we saw leaders emerge, finding and demonstrating qualities essential in those terrible moments. "How to be" qualities, not baskets of skills, rose in miraculous ways to comfort, to sustain, to challenge, to embrace a city in shock and sorrow. The mayor of New York City found these qualities, the spirit within, and inspired a city and a country; the governor of New York state rose to new heights of leadership as he provided essential support to a city and then, with the mayor, presented to the people the example of the indispensable team, essential for massive response to a massive tragedy. From the over 350 firefighters and 200 police officers who lost their lives when they went into the inferno to save others, to the police, doctors, nurses, thousands of volunteers, and heroes from all over the country, to the Pentagon and that field in Pennsylvania, we find leaders whose character and heroism inspired a nation. It was clear that theirs was not a job; they were called to do what they did—they were leaders of quality and character who responded to their times.

So as I examined what I had written and communicated in that other world now gone, I found that I believe even more passionately in the whys: the values, the principles, the beliefs that define who we are, what we believe, what we do, and how we work with others, our fellow travelers on a shared journey to leadership in an uncertain world.

CHAPTER 1

The "How to Be" Leader

CHIEF EXECUTIVE **MAGAZINE** asked a number of corporate chief executives "to look over the horizon of today's headlines," "size up the future," and describe the most pressing tasks that lie beyond the millennium for chief executives. I was invited to do so as well. In my response I wrote, "The three major challenges CEOs will face have little to do with managing the enterprise's tangible assets and everything to do with monitoring the quality of: leadership, the work force, and relationships." After the magazine came out, a corporate leader wrote to me and said, "Your comments make great sense to me. I believe that the three challenges you describe are like legs on a stool. Yet I see leaders attending to just one, or perhaps two, of the legs!"

In the tenuous years that lie ahead, the familiar benchmarks, guideposts, and milestones will change as rapidly and explosively as the times, but the one constant at the center of the vortex will be the leader. The leader beyond the millennium will not be the leader who has learned the lessons of *how to do it,* with ledgers of "hows" balanced with "its" that dissolve in the crashing changes ahead. The leader for today and the future will be focused on *how to be*—how to develop quality, character, mind-set, values, principles, and courage.

The "how to be" leader knows that people are the organization's greatest asset and in word, behavior, and relationships she or he demonstrates this powerful philosophy. This leader long ago banned the hierarchy and, involving many heads and hands, built a new kind of structure. The new design took people out of the boxes of the old hierarchy and moved them into a more circular, flexible, and fluid management system that released the energy and spirit of our people.

The "how to be" leader builds dispersed and diverse leadership—distributing leadership to the outermost edges of the circle to unleash the power of shared responsibility. The leader builds a work force, board, and staff that reflect the many faces of the community and environment, so that customers and constituents find themselves when they view this richly diverse organization of the future.

This "how to be" leader holds forth the vision of the organization's future in compelling ways that ignite the spark needed to build the inclusive enterprise. The leader mobilizes people around the mission of the organization, making it a powerful force in the uncertain times ahead. Mobilizing around mission generates a force that transforms the workplace into one in which workers and teams can express themselves in their work and find significance beyond the task, as they manage for the mission. Through a consistent focus on mission, the "how to be" leader gives the dispersed and diverse leaders of the enterprise a clear sense of direction and the opportunity to find meaning in their work.

The "how to be" leader knows that listening to the customer and learning what he or she values—"digging in the field"—will be a critical component, even more so in the future than today. Global and local competition will only accelerate, and the need to focus on what the customer values will grow stronger.

Everyone will watch tomorrow's leader, as we watch today's, to see if the business practices of the organization are consistent with the principles espoused by the leader. In all interactions, from the smallest to the largest, the behavior of the "how to be" leader will demonstrate a belief in the worth and dignity of the men and women who make up the enterprise.

Key to the societal significance of tomorrow's leaders is the way they embrace the totality of leadership, not just including "my organization" but reaching beyond the walls as well. The "how to be" leader, whether he or she is working in the private, public, or social sector, recognizes the significance of the lives of the men and women who make up the enterprise, the value of a workplace that nurtures the people whose performance is essential to furthering the mission, and the necessity of a healthy community to the success of an organization. The wise leader embraces all those concerned in a circle that surrounds the corporation, the organization, the people, the leadership, and the community.

The challenges presented from outside the walls will require as much attention, commitment, and energy as the most pressing tasks within. Leaders of the future will say, "This is intolerable," as they look at the schools, at the health of children who will make up the future workforce, at inadequate preparation for life and work in too many families, at people losing trust in their institutions. The new leaders will build the healthy community as energetically as they build the healthy, productive enterprise, knowing that the high-performance organization cannot exist if it fails its people in an ailing community.

Today's concerns about a lack of workers' loyalty to the corporation and a corresponding lack of corporations' loyalty to the workforce are sending a clear message to the leaders of tomorrow. The pit bulls of the marketplace may find that their slash-and-crunch and hang-on-till-death philosophies are as dead as the spirits of their troops. In the end, as organizations reduce their workforces, will it be the leader of a dispirited, demoralized workforce who leads the pack or will it be the new leader, guiding from vision, principle, and values, who builds trust and releases the energy and creativity of the work-force?

The great observers are not forecasting good times, but in the very hazards that lie ahead for leaders, remarkable opportunities exist for those who would lead their enterprises and this country into a new kind of community—a cohesive community of healthy children, strong families, good schools, decent neighborhoods, and work that dignifies. It is in this arena that leaders with new mind-sets and visions will forge new relationships, crossing all three sectors to build partnerships and community. This will take a different breed (or the old breed sloughing off the tired, go-it-alone approach), made up of leaders who dare to see life and community whole, who view work as an amazing opportunity to express everything within that gives passion and light to living, and who have the courage to lead from the front on the issues, principles, vision, and mission that become the star to steer by. Leaders of the future can only speculate on the tangibles that will define the challenges that lie ahead. But the intangibles, the leadership qualities required, are as constant as the North Star. They are expressed in the character, the power within, and the "how to be" of leaders beyond the millennium.

[1996]

CHAPTER 2

A Reason
to Believe

I SPOKE RECENTLY to an audience of university students, faculty, and community leaders. We had a vigorous question and answer period, and when people came up to talk afterward, one young man lingered on the sidelines. When everyone else had moved on, this college freshman said to me, "I wanted to ask you a question during the question and answer period, but I didn't want to embarrass you." I smiled and said, "Please, ask it now." He asked, "Why should I not be cynical?"

He went on to talk about a corporate leader who had donated a large amount of money (but a small fraction of his net worth) to charity. In the student's view, the leader had given to receive a big tax deduction and to get his name in the paper. "Why should I not be cynical?" he asked again. I told him, first, "I am never cynical. Even my blood type is B positive." He smiled, but his serious question deserved a serious answer.

I told him that I didn't know enough about that particular case to comment, but I asked if I could describe some corporate leaders I know who *have* made a difference. One is Bill Pollard, chairman of ServiceMaster, one of the most admired corporations in the world and the most successful service corporation in our country for twenty-five years. Bill Pollard devotes enormous energy and commitment to the development of his 240,000 employees. They mop floors in hospitals, serve food in college cafeterias, eliminate termites, take care of lawns and trees, and clean houses. He believes that every one of them is a person of great worth and dignity and that each deserves career development and learning opportunities. That is why some men and women who begin in basic cleaning services end up managing ServiceMaster business units.

Bill's investment in career development has nothing to do with tax breaks; it has everything to do with a belief that people truly are his organization's greatest asset, and he acts on that belief. He is forthright about his company's mission, which, appropriately enough, is inscribed on the wall of his headquarters: "To honor God in all we do, to help people develop, to pursue excellence, and to grow profitably." These aims can mean different things to different people. But it is a statement that cannot be taken lightly, and Pollard holds himself and his managers accountable to it. He mobilizes people around it.

I also told the young man about Tom Moran, president and CEO of Mutual of America. His company's community involvement—which includes investments of time, money, and management support to local community projects and nonprofit organizations—is an essential part of Mutual of America's culture. It has little to do with money because the return on investment, while highly significant in social terms, has little financial impact on a $10 billion corporation. But the impact on the company's 1,100 employees—over 97 percent of whom participate—and on the people of the community is tremendous. Tom's predecessor and current chairman of the board, William Flynn, made a statement I have heard from very few corporate leaders. He told employees, "The day we have to downsize, the day we have to eliminate jobs, my name will be the first on the list."

Finally, I talked about Lew Platt, former chairman of Hewlett-Packard. He was intent on reinventing and reenergizing a great corporation. Yet he remained passionate about building a richly diverse organization worldwide and promoting a healthy balance between work and life for employees. He saw that while a viable organization must be financially sound, it can grow in partnership with employees and communities, not at their expense.

Those of us in leadership positions must be able to answer the questions of skeptics—not with homilies but with real and positive examples of leaders in all three sectors who are build-ing healthy, cohesive organizations and communities. Those of us who have a forum for addressing constituents need to identify what Peter Drucker calls "islands of health and strength" in this country. There are thousands of them, and they matter to the eighteen-year-old students who ask the tough questions.

Young people are looking for evidence of values-driven leadership because they see too many examples of people in positions of authority who are self-serving, focused only on financial lines, or simply indifferent to others. We cannot af-ford to have young people answering for themselves, on the basis of a few negative examples, the question, "Why should I not be cynical?" We owe it to them to articulate real exam-ples of principled, effective leaders who understand and value the contributions of others. We also have to be clear about our own principles and values, grounded in everyday practice.

Young people reflect a society, a world, that is hungry for heroes. We need to look with new eyes and identify for our-selves the heroes around us. Heroes can be found throughout society—not in the person of the man on the white horse, but among men and women who know that the future is going to be different and who are themselves making a difference as they help to shape tomorrow. Today's heroes move beyond the walls of their enterprise and help build a better world. They provide an alternative to today's sober realities. They

Hesselbein on Leadership

hold a vision before us, a vision beyond what is, to what could be.

By the time we finished our conversation, the auditorium had emptied. I wanted to stay connected, and we agreed to keep in touch. I told him, "You are asking the right question. And your question is far more significant than my answer." He thanked me and walked slowly away, modest, quiet, and clearly weighing the evidence. I hope to hear how he answers his question for himself in the coming years. I know that his question was a great gift. It taught me much, and yet his question still haunts me.

[1999]

CHAPTER 3

Carry a Big Basket

L ONG AGO, when my first community involvement was leading Girl Scout Troop 17 in Johnstown, Pennsylvania, I met a wonderful woman at a training seminar for new leaders. When I mentioned to her that Jane, another new leader, said she was not getting anything out of the course, Rose responded with words straight from her southern mountain wisdom: "You have to carry a big basket to bring something home."

I was a young mother of a small boy at the time, and through all the years that followed I've remembered Rose's wisdom and language. I have carried big baskets made of many materials, of differing designs and shapes. Each basket bears a tag; the tags change with the context. Four leadership imperatives—innovation, inclusion, opportunity and equal access, and values-based management—merit their own tags. And mission focus, the leadership essential, guides us in how we use what we have gathered in our baskets on the journey home.

When I carry my innovation basket, there is no lid; it is wide open to the many dimensions of change and performance. (In fact, the tag hanging on my innovation basket is a definition by Peter Drucker: "Innovation: change that creates a new dimension of performance." The power of language to break barriers and unleash energy continually amazes.) Change is opportunity; I have a basket waiting to be filled with new ideas, straws in the wind, different partners and new practices, and a willingness to dump out the old and irrelevant to make room for new approaches. This flexible basket grows to contain all we need to keep leadership and organizations viable.

Another I am eager to carry (our baskets are never too heavy) is the basket tagged "inclusion." This one I grab with both hands for the ideas, models, and processes that create richly diverse organizations and spell relevance, continuity, and effectiveness. Building the inclusive, cohesive, vibrant institution does indeed require the biggest basket in town—for it has to have room for all of us. Not just the favored few, those who look alike and think alike, but all who are part of the community of the future. When equal access prevails, the synergy of inclusion propels us far beyond the old gated enclaves of the past into the richness of opportunities that lie beyond the walls.

When the opportunity tag hangs from my basket—and here we each define and redefine opportunity in our own terms—Emerson's call comes clearly across the centuries: "Be ye an opener of doors." In my opportunity basket, I pile the opportunity for every child to learn, of every man and woman to find work that dignifies and delights, the opportunity to move and travel and explore without fear, to seek opportunity not just for ourselves but for all others. Every day, this leadership imperative grows, multiplies, and invigorates. A big basket it is, but with each contribution it almost carries itself because the momentum of changed lives through new opportunities lifts both basket and carrier.

Every time I lift my values basket, I know it is a time of testing. I am very careful about what I put into and take out of this basket, for it holds who I am, why I do what I do, what motivates, guides, moves, and challenges me. The other baskets, too, are indispensable. But the values basket carries my beliefs, principles, spirit—the values I struggle to live by. Of all the baskets a leader carries this has the most profound meaning. In meeting the daily challenges of leadership, wherever we are in this tenuous life, work, and world, the values basket sustains and encourages us. The contents of this basket remind us that leadership is a matter of how to *be,* not how to *do* it, and that, in the end, it is the quality and the character of the leader that determine the performance, the results. This basket is woven from the innermost strands of our lives.

I happen to love baskets of all kinds, from anywhere in the world. We can study the baskets on our shelves and see the fine work, the design someone somewhere meticulously crafted for the receiver. Whether it is Hopi baskets from northern Arizona or Guatemalan art expressed with reeds or Kenyan precision in rushes, most baskets are still made by hand, by men and women and children far from where I am at this moment. So even the metaphorical receptacle for our thoughts, dreams, plans, frustrations carries a message about involvement, caring, and partnership.

The size of each basket is limited only by our own reluctance to lead fully, to lead from the front. They grow as our horizons expand until "limitless" becomes the best descriptor. If we practice planned abandonment the contents will be viable, relevant, and passionate even as our organizations and we grow and change. "Planned abandonment" is another lesson we learn from Peter Drucker and carry in our innovation basket. For if we are to remain mission focused, as we must if we are to be relevant in an uncertain age, then abandoning those things that do not further the mission is a leadership imperative.

For "mission focus" is stamped indelibly on each basket, on everything we carry, on the journey itself. If it doesn't further the mission, over the side it goes. Mission focus gets us where we want to go. For many leaders, the destination is a place where work, people, and challenge converge—mobilizing around mission, changing lives, building community, coming home. In these turbulent, often violent times, we recall with certitude that "it is the set of the sails and not the gales that determine the way we go." I don't know who wrote this in the treasured, obscure past, but the message illuminates the course to the future.

Great challenges, great opportunities, great ambiguities embrace us as we sort out what to carry, how to carry it, and with whom we travel. On this journey into the future, the small vision, the small scope, the small expectation, the small impact, the small basket is not for us. What we carry in our basket and what we bring home can change lives and build community. It can transform the organization and the society. In the end, we ourselves are transformed.

Carrying a big basket is a metaphor for living, for leading, perhaps even for the secret of a well-lived life. A long-ago observation from a then-young community leader who had discovered that learning was the great adventure comes whispering across the years: "You have to carry a big basket to bring something home."

[2002]

CHAPTER 4

Focus on
the Task

WHEN the great Duke Ellington wanted to describe a remarkable artist or an extraordinary work, he would say, "Beyond category." The phrase describes his own work as well—and offers a fitting definition of success in today's world. Ellington's words came to mind recently when a group of visiting management graduate students and faculty from Vienna asked my view of gender and organizational leadership.

Over luncheon, several graduate students who were women challenged: "Why are you the *chairman* of the Board of Governors of the Drucker Foundation—not the chairperson or chair?" I replied that this was simply a personal preference, that

I consider the word chairman a title derived from human, not *man*. On any board I chair, I am the chairman.

I use this rationale: Suppose there is a successful, well-led corporation, and I am chosen to follow its successful chairman who is a man. The first change I make is not going to be changing my title to chair or chairperson. If I assume the position, I assume the title. I acknowledged to the visitors that this is a view not commonly held—but that my preference is right for me and for my philosophy and leadership style.

As leaders who are women, we begin by acknowledging that we bring a special dimension to the work of our organization. Our contribution to furthering the mission is enhanced by our gender—any effective leader brings her life experience and point of view to bear. Diversity of gender, race, culture, and background in our leadership teams strengthens and enriches our organizations. But that is not the reason we, as leaders who are women, do what we do. The mission that defines why we do what we do has no gender.

Peter Drucker urges leaders to "focus on task, not gender." That advice serves us well. A focus on task is an imperative for all leaders who are working to build the richly diverse, inclusive, effective organization. Our increasingly diverse business, government, and social sector institutions reflect a sea change in American society, and our leaders' task is to make these institutions effective.

For seven years I served on the board of a large electric utility with eleven directors who were men. I served as this company was building two nuclear power plants. There is nothing more macho than a nuclear power plant. Yet in all of those meetings—ten times a year for seven years—I never walked into the boardroom thinking, "I Am Woman." I participated because I had something to contribute beyond gender. I never thought of myself as the woman on the board (though indeed I was); rather, I knew I brought a special perspective to the deliberations and the decisions.

Sometimes when I am being interviewed, a writer will say something such as, "We have read that yours is the ultimate in feminine management. Please describe your feminine management style." I reply that of course the observer observes what the observer observes, but that for me management is like money—it has no gender.

The management qualities that might be labeled feminine are embraced by remarkably effective women and men: leading with the power of language, cultivating relationships, building teams and structures that release the energy and potential of others, developing flexible and fluid management systems, building an inclusive organization that, in the words of Peter Drucker, "makes the strengths of their people effective and their weaknesses irrelevant." Some might call this feminine management, others would call it the enlightened way that we must, as Drucker says, "lead people and not contain them."

When I served a national organization designed to meet the special needs of girls and young women, I always hoped that there would come through all the work and content a consistent message. That message was, there is something marvelous about being a girl or a young woman, with remarkable opportunities that lie ahead, and we have to be prepared for them. I have not changed my philosophy. When we focus on task, our gender adds a special and positive dimension to all we do. In the new century, increasingly we will have enormous opportunities to be more significant than ever before. We choose our battles wisely.

Ten years ago I would not have written this chapter. It was a different world in the workplace, and the barriers to the talents of women were formidable. In the early nineties women and the corporate, government, and nonprofit leaders who supported equal access to opportunity, position, and significance were beginning a decade of remarkable progress. A growing number of women entered boardrooms, management teams, and key leadership positions. Women were ever more richly represented in business schools, law schools, and medical schools—opening doors that had been closed in the past and preparing themselves for future leadership. Many of the old issues were retired.

As we focus on task, we move beyond the old assumptions, practices, and language that can be barriers to equal access. One barrier is placing women in a special category of gender. If we see and describe ourselves as a "woman vice president," we may remain in a category never to be considered for the chief executive position.

The leadership challenges before us are basic, fundamental, and generic. The future calls us to lead beyond where we are, to focus on a new level of appreciation, inclusion, and performance. To continue to make remarkable progress, leaders who are women must focus on performance always. We must never forget the power of mission, values, and task. Peter Senge says that mission instills the passion and the patience for the long journey. It is a long journey but an exuberant one, because our traveling companions are men and women sharing a new vision of the future. We will achieve our vision only if we think and perform "beyond category."

[1999]

CHAPTER 5

The Power of Civility

LONG AGO, I heard Peter Drucker say, "Good manners are the lubricating oil of organizations." This was not Miss Manners or Emily Post speaking; it was the "father of modern management," the person who understands organization perhaps more clearly than any of us.

I silently cheered his message then, and I have been part of the cheering section on this issue ever since. The "tough" leaders of the past, who saved their manners for their social lives and believed in barking orders and the power of command and control, are now part of history.

In their place are leaders who demonstrate in language and behavior their appreciation and respect for the men and women of the enterprise. In these organizations, "Our people are our greatest asset" is more than a phrase. It is palpable in the culture.

Using the Tools of Leadership

Effective leaders today know that good manners are critical to success in workplace relationships, in team performance, in listening and responding to customers, and in managing a richly diverse workforce. Their good manners flow not from patterned niceness, but from genuine appreciation of their colleagues individually and the dignity of the work their colleagues do.

All of us have observed relationships marked by poor taste, bad manners, and a lack of civility. They are unproductive, they diminish both parties, and they often implode personally (or explode publicly) with predictable results. Just as one cannot have two sets of ethics—one for business and one for personal life—one cannot have two sets of manners.

How to Show Respect

As I was writing this piece I asked several friends to define good manners and civility. All had different answers but agreed in principle that manners have to do with rules of social behavior; civility has to do with respect for other people. Both are indispensable in building effective organizations. We acknowledge the humanity of the other person when we communicate at many levels that person's worth and dignity. Our behavior as well as our words build a climate of trust, a climate of respect, and a climate where mission, values, and equal access permeate the organization.

This is how we build the healthy, inclusive, and embracing relationships that unleash the human spirit. We can dismiss this as soft management and soft talk, but I challenge us to measure the performance of a team whose work is underscored by trust, civility, and good manners against a team where mistrust, disrespect, and lack of consideration are the rule of the day. No contest. Spirit, motivation, respect, and appreciation win every time. Dispirited, unmotivated, unappreciated workers cannot compete in a highly competitive world.

We now see leaders of the future who know that leadership has little to do with power and everything to do with responsibility. The dispersed leadership that marks a great organization starts with a shared commitment to mission and purpose. It is based on the clear delegation of tasks, and clear accountability for results. The energy, synergy, and productivity we count on to move the enterprise forward are determined by how people work together, by the example that we set every day. We have to demonstrate that attitude for ourselves before we can expect it in others.

In the rush to "reinvent" our organizations, or our communities, or ourselves, we sometimes overlook the time-tested principles that helped early great leaders succeed. We forget that long before "relationship marketing" or "unit of one" became buzzwords, leaders built genuine and felicitous relationships in work life, public life, and family life. The organization of the future will be relationship-centered, mission-focused, values-based, and demographics-driven. Good manners and civility are essential to the success of relationships across the organization, and will move to the front of the effective leader's portfolio.

In my work with CEOs who successfully manage the multiple demands and pressures of each day, I have found two attributes that help them build healthy relationships with others.

Knowing What's Important

Though they are usually the most heavily scheduled people in the organization, effective leaders never convey the impression that they are overwhelmed by their task. They always find time for people with an urgent problem or opportunity. And, invariably, they do more than talk; they live the message. Courtesy is their norm. They understand the power of civility, example, language, and persuasion.

The more effective the leaders are, the more they are able to make time for people and show genuine consideration for others. It is a graceful use of manners, the lubricating oil, to be sure. But it is also motivating and an effective way to work with people and, ultimately, "make their strengths effective and weaknesses irrelevant."

Too often we convey the message that we are rushed for time during an appointment, but if we focus on the person and what he or she brings, we send a very different message: that our time with that colleague—those fifteen or thirty minutes—

is the most important thing we can be doing at the moment. Listening to our internal customers is as important as listening to our external customers. Focus and attention convey genuine respect, which is the cornerstone of trust. It also helps us become more focused, organized, and in the end more productive.

Making Time Count

Like anything worthwhile, caring and respectful behavior takes time and effort. But in these demanding (and often uncivil) times, the question is not just how we balance our lives, it is how we balance our day. That balance requires discipline in how we use our time. It is, after all, what we do with our days, what choices we make, that defines our results as leaders, as men and women.

Every day has its priorities, its focus, and we have to concentrate on those. We often have to set aside things that are interesting to do but will not make a difference. We wake up determined that the day is not going to just happen to us. We know where we are going to invest our time, and with whom, how we shape and spend the day. Such discipline is not easy, but it's an exhilarating challenge of effective leadership.

In the end, leadership is all about valuing relationships, about valuing people. It is important to rise when someone enters our office, never look at our watch when we are talking with someone. Real etiquette is not about mindless or archaic ritual; it is about the quality and character of who we are. "Good manners" are the expression of genuine respect for others and for the task we share. They are critical to the success of the organization of the future.

As we hear from great leaders and thinkers from all sectors, in the journal articles, the book chapters, and the conferences of the Drucker Foundation and others, over and over from different voices, different minds, we hear hope for the future. We hear of a future where relationships are key and people are valued, where not just the task well performed but the life well lived is what counts. In the future, as now, living those values will be the challenge not just for the leader, but for us all.

[1997]

CHAPTER 6

Barriers to Leadership

L EADERSHIP has been my business for twenty-five years, with careers in Girl Scouting and now the Drucker Foundation. My messages on leadership always have been upbeat. Invitations to speak invariably have been on the challenges, visions, imperatives, or future of leadership. So when a group of Kellogg Foundation National Leadership Fellows asked me to address "Barriers to Leadership," I was a little taken aback. It was the only time I've been asked to address the negative aspects of the subject.

The request forced me to shift gears, to consciously distill what I had learned from experience but not yet articulated about barriers to leadership. From this introspection emerged two types of barriers: one personal and self-imposed, the other institutional, structural, or cultural.

Self-Imposed Barriers

1. Lack of formal, articulated personal goals and a road map of how to meet them. These should be written and close at hand, not just rolling around in your head.

2. No clear understanding of one's own strengths and areas to be strengthened (this calls for input from others, plus a plan for improving).

3. Believing that there is something called "business ethics," that there can be two standards: one for our personal lives and one for our professional lives.

4. Lack of generosity—not sharing ideas, time, encouragement, respect, compliments, and feedback with others—resulting in exactly the same treatment from them.

5. Leading from the rear—being tentative, fence sitting, never taking responsibility.

6. Always stressing what others can't do well rather than building on their strengths, what they do uncommonly well.

7. Playing "Chicken Little" instead of "The Little Engine That Could." Lack of positive approach to seri-

ous issues. Failing to present suggested solutions along with the problem.

8. Not taking charge of one's own personal learning and development.

Institutional Barriers

1. Hierarchical structures that restrict, constrict, box people in.

2. Corporate cultures that encourage mediocrity and reward playing it safe.

3. Corporate cultures and practices that kill the messenger.

4. Racism and sexism unacknowledged and unaddressed.

5. Fuzzy lines of accountability.

6. Lack of sharp differentiation between governance and management, and between policy and operations, with no clearly defined roles and responsibilities.

7. No mentoring plan for promising staff members.

8. Bottom-line mentality; not seeing people as the company's greatest asset.

9. Failing to build, now, a richly diverse, pluralistic organization that includes diversity on the board of directors and top management teams.

10. Not walking the talk; a leadership team whose behavior doesn't match its message.

11. Static staffing structures, with no job rotation or job expansion.

12. Lack of a formal, articulated plan for succession.

It takes courage for a leader to identify and confront self-imposed barriers, to put in place the personal strategies required to unleash the energy, innovation, and commitment to self-development. It takes equal courage to identify and confront the institutional barriers that limit and inhibit the people of the organization. And it takes real leadership to bulldoze the barriers—frequently time-honored, tradition-bound, deeply ingrained practices.

But when the barriers come down, the result is a competitive, productive, and motivated workforce focused on the future. Morale soars, performance rises, and the organization is liberated to reach its highest potential. Seeking out the barriers demands high intelligence; doing something about them demands managerial courage.

[1997]

CHAPTER 7

The Challenge of Leadership Transition

FEW EVENTS in the life of an organization are as critical, as visible, or as stressful as when the leader leaves the organization. The eyes of every employee, customer, partner, and investor are focused on the outgoing executive. How that moment is managed reveals the character and effectiveness of the leader, the organization, and its people. Leaders move into a new position with a strategy for capturing the promise and energy of a new beginning. To make a lasting difference, however, they must remember that an ending is also a beginning; it requires just as much thought and planning.

Leadership transition is an integral process for all leaders of an organization. It begins long before (and continues long after) the outgoing leader departs, and it presents a remarkable opportunity to move forward with a new understanding of the complexities, challenges, and changes the organization must address.

Unfortunately, the landscape of all three sectors—business, government, and social—is littered with the results of poorly planned and managed leadership transition. Diminished careers, disillusioned boards of directors, dysfunctional management teams, bewildered constituents, and all too frequently cynical public reaction flow from an inept transition.

Having served as CEO of four organizations, as chairman of the search committee of several others, and as a board member of a number of corporations and social sector organizations, I have participated in many leadership transitions. From these experiences I have learned how essential it is for the leader to begin well *and* to end well. Effective leaders plan an exit that is as positive and graceful as their entrance was. They come to the job committed to the mission and goals of the organization and to their personal goals, with a sense of where they want the organization to be and where they want to be personally when they leave. When those goals are realized, the transition to new leadership becomes a primary focus. It becomes, literally, the ultimate leadership responsibility.

Board Partnership

"Passing the baton" does not describe the dynamics of a successful transition. When leaders believe it is the best time for the organization's future and for their own, they plan, communicate, and manage the period of leadership transition. However, they manage the process; they do not select their successor. In partnership with the board, they involve all stakeholders and constituents appropriately. When well planned and well managed, the transition becomes a time of high morale and fulfilled expectations.

When I tell people that my year of leadership transition with the Girl Scouts of the USA was the most exuberant year in my career, they are incredulous. But it is true. I announced to the Girl Scouts board of directors on January 31, 1989, that I would be leaving January 31, 1990, and that together we would build a model of leadership transition. Many board and staff members could not believe that I would choose to leave at a time when things were going so well for the organization—but that was precisely the right time to leave. The transition process worked beautifully, and my last day on the job was as gratifying as my first.

Early in the transition year I bought copies of Thomas North Gilmore's *Making a Leadership Change,* the best book I know on the subject, for the management team and officers. The senior staff and I spent a one-day facilitated retreat preparing for our roles in the change of leadership. We talked about the future, not the past, and thought about the qualities needed for the management team in the years ahead. By the end of the day, no one doubted that I was leaving, and everyone was ready for the task ahead.

A Four-Step Process

In my experience, there are four critical phases of leadership transition.

Phase I: Defining a Vision

A search committee appointed by the board of directors, with superior staff support, describes its vision for the future of the organization and the major issues it will face in the next five to ten years. The vision statement is shared widely and describes both the nature of the organization ten years hence and the qualities required of the new chief executive to lead toward that vision. If the present leader and her team were right for yesterday and today, the new leader must be equally right for tomorrow. Celebration of the future—not perpetuation of the past—underscores all communication.

Phase II: Building a Search Infrastructure

The search committee selects a search firm that understands the vision, goals, and expectations of the organization. The chemistry has to be right. The chief executive designs and manages the process—not the search itself. She helps to articulate organizational goals, may offer insight on the qualities necessary in a successor, and may advise on the selection of a search firm. She provides superb staff support to the search committee, but then is scrupulous about not even appearing to direct the committee's work.

Phase III: Delegating Authority

The board of directors has delegated to the search committee the selection of the search firm. Board and staff members, and other constituents, should submit nominations to the search firm, *not* to the search committee, for screening—thus avoiding any appearance of internal pressure or preference. But before responsibility is delegated by the board of directors to the search committee, it is important for the board to agree on the selection process. Will the search committee present one final candidate to the board for approval, or does the board wish to interview two or three finalists? Once the selection process has been approved by the board, the delegation of authority must be clear and specific. The plan must then be adhered to as the process moves ahead.

Phase IV: Conducting the Search

The search committee and the search firm agree on the ways to work: whether, for example, to cast a wide net or to concentrate on particular fields; the timetables and deadlines to meet; the number of final candidates the committee will interview, and when and where they will be interviewed. Ethical behavior and observance of total confidentiality are key to the recruitment process. Ideally, the incoming leader will be able to work with the outgoing leader in the weeks or months before taking office—always observing that the present leader carries full responsibility for the organization until the day she leaves. There are no lame ducks in a successful transition.

These four steps are not a blueprint for the success of all searches, but they do suggest order and principle in what can be a stressful event. Not all partings are planned or voluntary, of course. In these cases, a generous and graceful separation can relieve some of the organizational anxiety.

Leaders spend much time thinking about how to propel the enterprise—and their careers—into the future. They usually spend far too little time thinking about the right time and way to leave. Yet a successful transition can be a seamless, productive, and unifying experience. Most of us will be remembered, in work and in life, for just a few words or deeds that made a difference to others. The way we choose to say good-bye is likely to be one of the ways we are remembered. If we execute our final leadership responsibility with the same care and attention that we gave to the first, our departure can be an inspiring gift to the enterprise and to the people in it.

[1997]

PART II

Leading the Organization of the Future

WHEN WE LISTEN to the spirit within, when we are called to lead—as all effective leaders are—we are leaders of change, not the protectors and perpetuators of a cherished, honored past. Leading the organization of the future in turbulent, tenuous times makes new demands on leaders: banning the hierarchy, building new and inclusive structures and systems that release the energies of our people, challenging the gospel of the status quo, and finding the leadership language that mobilizes our people around mission, innovation, and diversity. And leadership in these times means scanning the environment for those few trends that will have the greatest impact on the enterprise—identifying those few straws in the wind, not yet trends, that may change our direction.

The future calls with insistence, and leaders who are passionate about building the viable and relevant organization of the future lead their people with vision, mission, values, and beliefs that permeate the total organization. "We manage for the mission, we manage for innovation, we manage for diversity" describes how the leader of the future presents, directs, leads, and defines the management of the organization of the future. And this is the organization that will be present when the roll is called in 2010.

CHAPTER 8

Managing in a World That Is Round

FIVE HUNDRED YEARS AGO, Renaissance Man discovered that the world was round. Three hundred fifty years later, Organization Man developed the practice of management. But as this practice evolved, he forgot that his world was round, and he built a management world of squares and boxes and pyramids. His world had a special language that matched its structure: the language of command and control, of order and predict, of climb the ladder, of top and bottom, up and down, superior and subordinate.

In every large organization for the next one hundred years, rank equaled authority. And for the most part, the old hierarchy that boxed people and functions in squares and rectangles, in rigid structures, worked well. It even developed the famous pyramid with the CEO sitting on the pointed top, looking down as his workforce looked up.

And then a period of massive historic change began, of global competition and blurred boundaries, of old answers that did not fit the new realities. In all three sectors of public, private, and social sector organizations there grew a new cynicism about our basic institutions. With government, corporations, and voluntary or social sector organizations trying to ride the winds of change, a different philosophy began to move across the landscape of organizations, and with it came a new language, a new approach, and a new diversity of leadership.

In the 1970s and 1980s, some leaders in the private and the voluntary sectors saw that the hierarchies of the past did not fit the present they were living or the future they envisioned—so they took people and functions out of the boxes and, in doing so, they liberated the human spirit and transformed the organization.

Today we begin to see the new leaders, the leaders of the future, working in fluid and flexible management structures; and we hear a new language from these leaders—they understand the power of language.

> "Mission-focused, values-based, demographics-driven"

> "Learning to lead people and not to contain them"

> "Management is a tool—not an end"

> "Followership is trust"

From my own experience in 1976, when I left the mountains of western Pennsylvania to begin my work as CEO of Girl Scouts of the USA, the largest organization for girls and women in the world, I knew that the old structures were not right for the next decade, let alone the next century. So volunteers and staff together unleashed our people through a flat, circular, fluid management system (see Figure 8.1). In the new organizational structure, people and functions moved across three concentric circles, with the CEO in the middle looking across, not at the top looking down. Five minutes after it was presented, a colleague dubbed it "the bubble chart" and an observer, "the wheel of fortune." Our people moved across the circles of the organization—never up and down—and the result was high performance and high morale.

I am often asked by management students and middle managers in organizations I work with, "How can we free up the organization and make the changes you talk about if we are not at the top?" I reply, "You can begin where you are, whatever your job. You can bring a new insight, new leadership to your team, your group."

That advice applies equally—or especially—to senior executives. As Peter Senge points out in "The Ecology of Leadership" on page 18 of *Leader to Leader* (Fall 1996, issue number 2), when it comes to sustaining meaningful change, senior executives have considerably less power than most people think. But one place where they can effect change is with their own work groups and everyday activities.

Figure 8.1 The Wheel of Fortune

Forget boxes and pyramids. The organization chart in a circular management system has a center, but no top or bottom.

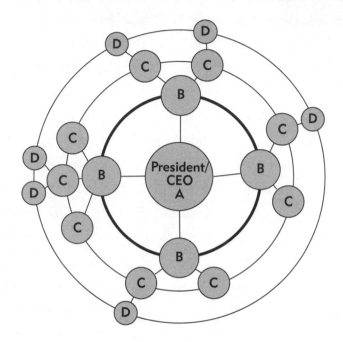

A: President and/or CEO
B: Vice President(s) for Management Unit (Management Circle)
C: Group Directors
D: Team Directors

With the return of a more fluid, circular view of the world, the days of turf battles, the star system, and the Lone Ranger are over. The day of the partnership is upon us. Leaders who learn to work with other corporations, government agencies, and social sector organizations will achieve new energy, new impact, and new significance in their organization's work. But to manage effective partnerships, leaders will have to master three imperatives—managing for the mission, managing for innovation, and managing for diversity.

Managing for the mission. Understanding one's mission is the essence of effective strategy, for the small nonprofit enterprise or the Fortune 500. Consider the power of three questions that Peter Drucker offers those who are formulating an organizational mission:

What is our business/mission?

Who is our customer?

What does the customer value?

We devoted many pages of the first issue of *Leader to Leader* to the power of a motivating, aligned mission, so I'll add just a simple observation. Peter Drucker says an effective mission statement "must fit on a T-shirt." I would add it must give people a clear, compelling, and motivating reason for the organization's existence. For example, "To serve the most vulnerable," the mission of the International Red Cross, satisfies both criteria and succeeds brilliantly; "To maximize shareholder value," the de facto mission of many corporations, satisfies only the first, and fails miserably.

Managing for innovation. Peter Drucker defines innovation as "change that creates a new dimension of performance." If we build innovation into how we structure the organization, how we lead the workforce, how we use teams, and how we design the ways we work together, then innovation becomes a natural part of the culture, the work, the mind-set, the "new dimension of performance." At the same time, we must practice "planned abandonment" and give up programs that may work today but will have little relevance in the future.

Managing for diversity. Perhaps the biggest question in today's world is, "How do we help people deal with their deepest differences?" Every leader must anticipate the impact of an aging, richly diverse population on the families, work organizations, services, and resources of every community. Headlines and TV tell us that governance amid diversity is the world's greatest challenge.

Those headlines also remind us of the grinding reality that no single entity—whether, public, private, or nonprofit—can restore our cities to health or create a healthy future for all our citizens. But in the emerging partnerships across all three sectors, we see remarkable openness and results. We need thousands more such partnerships. All of us are learning from one another. Thousands of dedicated public sector employees overcome daunting odds every day to improve their corner of the world. A huge social sector—with over a million voluntary organizations in the United States and over twenty million worldwide—shows what dedicated people can do, even on woefully inadequate budgets. And the incredible resources, energy, and expertise of the private sector reminds us that behind every problem there really is an opportunity. It is the leader's job to identify the critical issues in which his or her organization can make a difference, then build effective partnerships based on mission, innovation, and diversity to address those issues.

We need to remember that we can do little alone and yet much together. To be effective, leaders must look beyond the walls of the corporation, the university, the hospital, the agency—and work to build a cohesive community that embraces all its people—knowing there is no hope for a productive enterprise within the walls if the community outside the walls cannot provide the healthy, energetic workforce essential in a competitive world.

[1996]

CHAPTER 9

A Traveler Along the Road

T HE REVEREND Martin Luther King Jr. liked to tell this story: Centuries ago, there were two travelers on a dangerous road. Seeing a man needing help, there was the traveler who asked, "What will happen to me if I stop to help?" And the other traveler asked, "What will happen to him if I do not stop?"

We call the second traveler the Good Samaritan. Peter Drucker adds to the story that the next day, the Good Samaritan went back to check on the man. The Samaritan was focused on results.

Today the same questions are being asked. Again, there are the travelers who go hurriedly on their way, concerned only with self. Then there are those who are called to stop, to serve, to make a difference. In this century, we call them volunteers—traveling on a journey of hope, finding meaning and significance in service.

But in today's knowledge organizations, as Peter Drucker also reminds us, *everyone* is a volunteer. Most of us have the tools, which we carry in our heads, and the experience and desire to contribute. More and more, *we* choose the organization—the cause—with which to affiliate; leaders of organizations compete for the hearts and minds of people who want to be engaged. When everything in organizations and the world around us seems to be in question, certain things must remain fixed, and it is the leader's job to articulate those: why we do the work we do, what is important, and how we can make a difference.

A Mission of Care

That is what I mean when I counsel leaders to "manage for the mission." We must create organizations in which people know that it is their job not only to care for a traveler on the road—a customer, colleague, or community member who needs assistance—but to care about the results. To that end, nonprofit organizations are teaching business leaders ways to mobilize the talents and aspirations of volunteers and to define a mission that focuses their energies. And the private sector is teaching government and nonprofit leaders ways to organize for and measure results.

No longer can any organization get by with good intentions alone. Customers, clients, investors, donors, communities, and volunteers themselves all have a right to see a return on the time, money, and effort expended. People know that pursuing a mission without achieving results is dispiriting; achieving results without a mission is meaningless.

Learning to Lead

But if a sense of mission calls us all, it does so in different ways from the past. As never before, leaders need to be both constant learners and effective teachers. As Bob Galvin has said, "The development of leaders and of lifelong learners are so intertwined that they must be addressed together." Just as we look beyond the walls of our enterprise for new ways to collaborate and organize, we must look for new sources of learning and leadership.

The late Father John Culkin, Jesuit educator and author, wrote about film as an educational tool. He asked a seven-year-old to define education. The young boy replied, "Education is how kids learn stuff." It's the best definition I know, and it is the challenge to all of us engaged in leadership development.

How do we learn and teach the stuff of leadership? How do we make the new technology our own, using every learning and teaching tool to give our organizations the educational edge the future requires? Some of what we will learn in the difficult period ahead will be distilled from leadership lessons of present and past exemplary leaders. Much of what we will learn and teach, we will invent. How we will do it is still beyond the horizon, so we will learn to learn from one another. Today the stuff of leadership learning is flowing freely across corporations, social sector organizations, and government agencies. It is an exchange of information, ideas, and innovation that can begin to address the unprecedented needs of today's world. It is the task of leaders to open themselves and their institutions to that flow of ideas.

The Ultimate Discipline

Peter Drucker tells us that innovation is a discipline, not the inscrutable magic of a genius. Innovation, he says, "is not being brilliant, it's being conscientious." It comes from the same rigorous style of leadership that articulates the one area where we—individually and organizationally—can make a unique contribution. To be effective, leaders in every sector of the economy must concentrate on their niche—what they do uncommonly well—constantly reassess their performance, and, most difficult of all, be prepared to abandon what doesn't work and retain only those policies, programs, and practices that further the mission. Planned abandonment is the ultimate management discipline.

We need to move beyond the walls of the corporation, the agency, the organization, and build community with the same energy and commitment we invested to build the enterprise within the walls. Moving beyond the walls is not a matter of altruism; it is enlightened self-interest, a business necessity. No one can afford to neglect the forces operating around us, or to ignore the people we sell to, buy from, hire, and serve. Leaders in every field know that we cannot do anything—construct homes, write software, educate the young—without the help of others.

Our organizations need leaders who know how to plan in tenuous times. Leaders who can work in alliance and collaboration, and assure that board, staff, and the workforce reflect the demographics of the community. Leaders who know that this is the time to let the little things go—and focus on the few big things that will shape the future. Leaders who know that significance and diversity are synonymous—that the strategic context is as significant as the strategic design.

At the Drucker Foundation 1997 conference "Innovation: Mastering the Tools of Change," Peter Senge told us, "Mission instills the passion and patience for the long journey." If we can summon both the passion to pursue that journey and the patience to stop for the travelers we meet along the way, our organizations will be well served indeed.

[1998]

CHAPTER 10

Journey to Transformation

IN A WORLD where the rules are constantly changing, millions of people in every sector of the economy are wrestling with the new demands of leadership. I hear managers everywhere discussing the same fundamental challenge—the journey to transformation, moving from where we are to where we want to be in the tenuous future that lies before us. Around the world, in universities, the community of faith, corporations, government, and the burgeoning social sector, leaders are working to shape the transformation of their institutions.

I traveled to Stockholm, where I worked with the national board, staff, and chapter volunteers of the Swedish Red Cross and spoke to members of the business community, voluntary organizations, and the press. There were no barriers, no management terms to be explained, no awkward moments—only easy translations of: "walk the talk," "listen to the customer," "manage for the mission," "dispersed leadership."

In sharing experiences across the public, private, and social sectors, I have found that organizations usually pass eight milestones to reach their destination—a relevant, viable, effective organization. These milestones are as relevant to the Swedish Red Cross, or the Girl Scouts, as to a large business or government agency.

1. *Scan the environment.* Through reading, surveys, interviews, and so on, we identify the major trends likely to affect the organization. The essence of strategy is to define the implications of those trends. Sometimes we can catch a straw in the wind and have a responsive program or project ready as the trend emerges—not after. This assessment of emerging trends and implications, supplemented by internal data, provides essential background for planning change—and offers a better basis for action than our own preconceptions. Flying on assumptions can be fatal.

2. *Revisit the mission.* At the Drucker Foundation we review our mission every three years, and refine it if necessary. The foundation is over twelve years old, and we've revisited and refined our mission four times—not because we couldn't get it right the first time, with Peter Drucker in the room, but

because the environment and the needs of our customers had changed.

The mission statement should simply explain why we do what we do, our reason for being—our purpose. Knowing management is a tool, not an end, we manage not for the sake of managing in its own right, but for the mission. And one's mission does not define how one manages but simply why. It must be clear, powerful, compelling, and to the point. The mission of the International Red Cross—"To serve the most vulnerable"—is a perfect example of clarity and power.

When we revisit the mission we ask ourselves the three classic questions Peter Drucker has been helping corporations answer for over fifty years:

- What is our mission?

- Who is our customer?

- What does our customer value?

When we answer these, we are well on our way to managing for the mission.

3. *Ban the hierarchy.* Transformation requires moving people out of their organizational boxes into flexible, fluid management systems. We cannot continue to put people into little squares on a structure chart. Psychologically it boxes them in. I prefer circles—concentric circles of functions and

positions in a staffing design that looks almost organic (see "Managing in a World That Is Round," Chapter Eight). Job rotation becomes an enriching reality. People move in circular ways—learning new skills, expanding positions. We need to ban a hierarchy not suited to today's knowledge workers, "who carry their tool kits in their heads."

4. *Challenge the gospel.* There should be no sacred cows as we challenge every policy, practice, procedure, and assumption. In transforming themselves, organizations must practice "planned abandonment"—discarding programs, policies, and practices that work today but have little relevance to the future and the organization we are building to meet that future. We challenge the status quo.

5. *Employ the power of language.* Leaders must beam a few clear, consistent messages over and over. They must lead by voice, communicating with all their customers, all their constituents, a few powerful messages that connect and illuminate. When, for example, Max De Pree led his company, Herman Miller, to world leadership, he spoke about workers needing "a covenant, not a contract." Such powerful aspirations—and the language to go with them—are essential to guide an organization into transformation.

6. *Disperse leadership across the organization.* Every organization must have not one but many leaders. Some speak of "empowerment," others of "sharing the tasks of leadership." I think of it as dispersing leadership—with leaders developed

and performing across every level of the organization. Leadership is a responsibility shared by all members of the organization.

7. *Lead from the front, don't push from the rear.* The leader of the future does not sit on the fence, waiting to see which way the wind is blowing. The leader articulates clear positions on issues affecting the organization and is the embodiment of the enterprise, of its values and principles. Leaders model desired behaviors, never break a promise, and know that leadership is a matter of how to be, not how to do it.

8. *Assess performance.* Self-assessment is essential to progress. From the beginning of the change process, we are clear about mission, goals, and objectives. Well-defined action steps and a plan for measuring results are essential to planning any organizational change. We then can embark upon the journey with goals and measures in place. At the end of the process, the most exuberant phase of the journey, we evaluate our performance and celebrate the transformation.

Across the globe, for leaders living in tenuous times, the journey to transformation is a journey into an uncertain future. These leaders are taking today's organization and transforming it into tomorrow's productive, high-performance enterprise. While the milestones on the journey are known, the destinations are uncharted, and for each organization the destination will be determined not only by the curve of the road ahead but also by the power of the mission and the leadership it inspires.

[1998]

CHAPTER 11

Putting One's House in Order

TODAY MORE THAN EVER, we need to put our house in order. In fact, some people believe the house is on fire. Over many years all organizations, especially long-established ones, accumulate outmoded practices, policies, and procedures; the leader's job is to take stock, assess our organizational estate, and discard what no longer works. Clearing the cobwebs from this old house is an adventure in "planned abandonment."

We know that the future demands a new approach to planning, and to leading change. "Business as usual" is dead. Vision, mission, and courage will carry the day.

To move from vision to action, to lead vibrant organizations that can flourish in the 2000s, consider an exercise that for generations has helped people refresh and renew their lives: spring house cleaning. A passionate western Pennsylvania value (my roots are showing), this practice is invaluable in the life of an organization and its leaders.

Three Dimensions of Change

For today's organizations, cleaning the attic—"getting one's house in order"—means, first of all, revisiting one's mission: the short, powerful, compelling statement of why the organization does what it does, its reason for being. From a passionate, relevant mission flow the few powerful goals that reflect the organization's vision of the future. And from those goals flow the objectives, action steps, and organizational tactics that will carry the enterprise forward. We ask the five classic questions that Peter Drucker has charged organizations to answer for the past sixty years: What is our mission? Who is the customer? What does the customer value? What are our results? What is our plan?

But creating this organizational coherence is just the first imperative of change. The second dimension of good housekeeping is the plan for the *leadership* of the organization. Preparing our leadership house for the future requires as much time, energy, and rigor as the strategic plan for the enterprise itself.

To create a plan for the leadership corps we must ask ourselves several more questions. These include:

- What are our leadership strengths?

- What are the areas to be strengthened?

- Are we leading from the front? Do we anticipate change and articulate shared aspirations, or simply react to crises?

- How do we deploy our leaders, our teams, our people to further the mission and achieve our goals?

- Do we use job expansion, job rotation, and opportunities for development in innovative ways to release the energies of people and increase job satisfaction?

- Do our leaders see themselves as the embodiment of the mission, values, and beliefs of the organization?

- How can we sharpen communication skills and attitudes—knowing communication is not merely saying something, it is being heard?

- Are we building today the richly diverse, inclusive, cohesive organization that our vision and mission and the future demand?

The answers to these questions help us build effective teams, allocate appropriate resources, and develop energetic leaders in response to powerful goals and objectives.

The third dimension of change—getting our *personal* house in order—is perhaps the most challenging, and most neglected. It requires reserving the time, building the psychic energy, for introspection. When society is transformed, the organization is transformed, and in the end, we ourselves are transformed. We play an active role in all three.

Just as leaders are responsible for understanding their organization's strengths and preparing for its future, we must assess our personal strengths and take responsibility for planning our own development. For each of us, this will require listening to the whispers of our lives. We look at the intensely personal challenges of our health, our well-being, our relationships with others, and the promptings of our spiritual life—however we define it.

Bringing the Search Home

From such reflection we can set the goals of our own work—for instance, work-life balance—and ensure that our lives are consistent with the values and mission of the organization we are building. In our personal plan we are responsible for our own development, with checkpoints along the way.

I recently talked with a highly successful CEO who shared with me his plan for 2010—he called it his "learning journey." It included fewer "things to do," greater focus, and more time for writing and for family—and specified deadlines for action. This went far beyond the business plan for a successful organization; it was the personal plan for a successful life.

When we align the organization's plan for the future with the plan for its leadership and with our own personal plan, they become one: the powerful symbol of the integrated, innovative organization of the future and its leaders. We look to other leaders, past or present, whose personal vision and values were congruent with the credo, the values of their organization. For instance, James Burke, former CEO of Johnson & Johnson, continues to inspire and motivate through his example, his results, his legacy.

Effective leaders have learned that moving from vision to reality requires a road map, a business plan for the future. When we create a vision for the institution, its leadership, and ourselves, we create a new house. We have left behind business as usual in all we see and do. It is an exuberant journey. It is called managing the dream.

[2000]

CHAPTER 12

The One Big Question

WHEN ORGANIZATIONS in every sector of society begin asking the same question at the same time, something is up. The question—raised with increasing frequency by leading public, private, and nonprofit organizations—is, How do we develop the leaders our organizations require for an uncertain future?

As corporations, governments, and social sector organizations move toward ever more turbulent times, there is one imperative—leadership development—that will make a vital difference. It is no longer a theoretical issue; urgent conversations in boardrooms around the world make clear that the viability of our institutions in a new century is a universal, very real concern.

I listen closely to these conversations and sometimes have the good fortune to take part in them. I have had a number of remarkable meetings with business and social sector CEOs, U.S. Army generals, state and federal elected officials, scholars, and public service interns and fellows. In every case, they share the belief that no investment in the tangible assets of an organization can equal an investment in its greatest asset—leaders at every level who will define new dimensions of performance, new clarity, new commitment to the vision and mission of the organization.

That shared belief was underscored in a meeting with a group finely attuned to the value of the greatest asset: fourteen human resource executives for leading financial and other corporate institutions. All were working to address the limited supply of effective leaders in organizations in their field. The current strategy was to simply raid the talent of a competitor. Some of their companies, and many others, were saying, in effect, that it's more expedient to lure talent from others than to develop and invest in the people they already had. They felt this was a sad statement—and in the long term a losing strategy. It does nothing to expand the talent pool, and ultimately it assures you of losing your own talent to a higher bidder. And these corporate leaders were quickly coming to the realization that it does no good to build offices, buy computers, and develop new services unless you have the people to grow the organization.

A financial leader of global renown, World Bank President James Wolfensohn reached similar conclusions. Seeing the need to transform the world's largest international development agency—an organization with $162 billion in assets and ten thousand employees—he started not with systems or policies but with people. He looked to the organization's incumbent leadership and staff to transform the organization. To encourage change, he assigned Washington-based managers to field offices around the world, bringing in speakers from diverse fields, and sending top managers to a six-week, custom-designed management training program. As he stated in *Barron's:* "I'm trying to encourage people to look beyond their past experience. . . . The World Bank has the talent in-house to become the world's premier expert on development."

Leaders Develop Leaders

To develop others requires leaders' significant personal effort in identifying the qualities, skills, and attitudes for leading beyond the horizon. It also requires the courage to challenge the old assumptions, the old answers, the old structures that supported yesterday's leaders. Peter Drucker reminds us that organizations exist to make peoples' strengths effective and their weaknesses irrelevant. And this is the work of effective leaders. Drucker also tells us that "there may be 'born leaders,' but there are surely far too few to depend on them." The future leadership team—the core contributors ready for the challenge of rigorous leadership development—is dispersed throughout your organization now.

Consider the U.S. Army, with its superb record of developing leaders. It is one of the most innovative training organizations in the world, but its leaders do not believe they have all the answers. Recently, former Army chief of staff General Dennis J. Reimer brought together several generals and CEOs from business for a two-day conference to share ideas on developing military leaders for the next century.

This gathering of remarkably diverse, accomplished leaders was a case study of synergy—what can happen when you assemble different minds and varied experiences to work on a common challenge. One outcome of this and all the similar sessions in which I have participated was the recognition that developing future leaders requires an investment of today's leaders' time and resources. It takes both rigorous questioning of what are we doing now to develop our people and the willingness to invest today for future relevance. Leadership development is a regular part of the activities of successful corporate leaders.

Dedication to the development of people is also the hallmark of some social sector organizations. For example, the leaders of a major voluntary organization were not satisfied with the analytical, presentation, and managerial skills of their young executives. They asked a Harvard Business School faculty team to develop a corporate management program for the organization's executive staff. Two years later the executives of this community-based organization looked, sounded, and performed with great self-confidence and high effectiveness. The symbolism—the organization's investment in a world-class executive development program, with the message that only the best was good enough for those who would lead the organization in the future—was as powerful as the learning opportunity itself.

Five Questions for the Future

Anxiety about the uncertain future is pervasive in today's organizations. But I see leaders in all three sectors reaching into the organization and out to their customers and community, reaffirming their values, and reexamining their mission. Such reflection is the first step in developing others because, before we can define the kinds of leadership we will need in 2010, we have to describe what our organization will look like in the future. We have to ask such questions as:

- What new demands will we face?

- What will be different about our customers?

- Who will be our customers?

- What can we do that will make the biggest difference, and what is the one thing that we must do for anything else to happen?

- What qualities of the new leader will best match the vision of our organization in the future?

The U.S. Army, for example, believes that we are entering not just a new century, but a very different era—an era in which a combination of time-tested leadership practices will remain viable but will need to be augmented with new leader competencies. Another reality that the Army's leaders must ponder is the role of a smaller army in a more diverse society, one in which fewer people have military experience. They understand that the context of the world we operate in is as important as the content of the services we provide. And the context for the U.S. Army–CEO conference was Gettysburg—site of the bloodiest battle in our history. We walked the battlefield, and, with the help of an Army historian, learned what those generals were thinking in 1863 and what happened to the 150,000 young men they asked to stand and give their lives for a cause. It was a powerful experience that had everything to do with the training of future leaders.

For the Army, the question is, If the twenty-first century is going to be different, then what kind of leadership does the Army need to provide? The answer to that question must also have a context—the organization's mission, its reason for being. I shared with General Reimer that West Point's mission statement, "To provide to the country leaders of character, to serve the common defense," is one of my two favorites in the world. Like the mission statement of the International Red

Cross ("to serve the most vulnerable"), it provides a short, powerful, compelling statement of why the organization exists.

How do we develop the leaders our organizations require for an uncertain future? We see effective responses to this question as leaders across all three sectors move from wisdom to action. They each answer this tough question with action today and make a commitment to the future. Perhaps most important, they behave as though the people of the organization were indeed its most valuable asset, and they invest their attention and money in building that resource. They are developing the leaders of the future, not simply to survive today, but to further the mission far beyond tomorrow.

[1998]

CHAPTER 13

When the Roll
Is Called in 2010

I WAS STRUGGLING to write this article about what leaders and organizations must do, today, to be viable and relevant ten years from now. I told Rob Johnston, our president, that I thought the title would be "When the Roll Is Called in 2010." He left and shortly returned to my office with a Web site printout of a great old hymn I remember from my Methodist Sunday School days: "When the Roll Is Called Up Yonder, I'll Be There." That wasn't exactly what I had in mind.

My concern is with how our actions today shape our legacy. Building a sustainable organization is one of a leader's primary responsibilities. When the challenges of today have been met, will your organization have the vigor to grow tomorrow? When the roll is called in 2010, will your organization be present?

Few social observers project that the years 2002–2010 will be easy ones for organizations in the public, private, and social sectors. Instead, *tenuous, turbulent,* and *tough* are the descriptors I hear when thought leaders evoke the future. But *inclusive, wide open,* and *promising* are part of the picture as well.

To meet the challenges and opportunities of the years to come requires hard work. My checklist—not for survival but for a successful journey to 2010—includes the following check points:

√ Revisiting the mission in 2003, 2006, and 2009, each time refining or amending it so that it reflects shifts in the environment and the changing needs of changing customers as part of a formal self-assessment process.

√ Mobilizing the total organization around mission, until everyone including the newest secretary and the worker on the loading dock can tell you the mission of the enterprise—why it does what it does, its reason for being, its purpose.

√ Developing no more than five powerful strategic goals that, together, are the board's vision of the desired future of the organization.

√ Focusing on those few initiatives that will make a difference—not skimming the surface of an overstuffed list of priorities. Focus is key.

√ Deploying people and allocating resources where they will have an impact, that is, only where they can further the mission and achieve the few powerful goals.

√ Practicing Peter Drucker's "planned abandonment": jettisoning current policies, practices, and assumptions as soon as it becomes clear they will have little relevance in the future.

√ Navigating the many streams of venture philanthropy, whether gearing up for the "ask" or as a philanthropist seeking to make an investment in changing the lives of people by partnering with a social sector organization.

√ Expanding the definition of communication from saying something to being heard.

√ Providing board members and the entire staff and workforce with carefully planned continuing learning opportunities designed to increase the capacity and unleash the creative energy of the people of the organization.

√ Developing the leadership mind-set that embraces innovation as a life force, not as a technological improvement.

- ✓ Structuring the finances of the organization—whether as seeker or funder in the social sector, business, or government—so that income streams are focused on the few great initiatives that will change lives, build community, and make a measurable difference.

- ✓ Transforming performance measurement into a management imperative that moves beyond the old forms and assumptions and toward creative and inclusive approaches to "measuring what we value and valuing what we measure."

- ✓ Scanning the environment and identifying major trends and implications for the organization in preparation for riding the wave of rapidly changing demographics.

- ✓ Building a mission-focused, values-based, demographics-driven organization.

- ✓ Planning for leadership transition in a thoughtful way. Leaving well and at the right moment is one of the greatest gifts a leader can give to the organization.

- ✓ Grooming successors—not a chosen one but a pool of gifted potential leaders. This is part of the leader's daily challenges.

- ✓ Making job rotation and job expansion into widespread organizational practices that are part of planning for the future.

√ Dispersing the tasks of leadership across the organization until there are leaders at every level and dispersed leadership is the reality.

√ Leading from the front, with leaders the embodiment of the mission and values in thinking, action, and communication.

√ Recognizing technology not as driver but as tool. Changing the technology as needs change, not changing needs and style to match the tool. Shaping the future, not being shaped by it.

√ Permeating every job, every plan with a marketing mind-set. Marketing means being close to the customer and listening and responding to what the customer values.

√ Building on strengths instead of dwelling on weaknesses until the organization has succeeded in, as Peter Drucker says, "making the strengths of our people effective and their weaknesses irrelevant."

√ Throwing out the old hierarchy and building flexible, fluid, circular management systems with inclusive leadership language to match.

√ Allocating funds for leadership development opportunities and resources for all the people of the enterprise.

√ Developing the richly diverse organization so that

board, management team, staff, employees, faculty, administration, and all communications materials reflect the diversity of the community, and we can respond with a resounding yes to the critical question: "When they look at us, can they find themselves?"

√ Making every leader—every person who directs the work of others—accountable for building the richly diverse team, group, or organization.

√ Keying individual performance appraisals to organizational performance.

√ Governance is governance. Management is management. Sharply differentiating the two by delineating clear roles, responsibilities, and accountabilities, resulting in a partnership of mutual trust and purpose. Building the partnership on open communication, adopting the philosophy of no surprises.

√ Using a common leadership and management language within the organization and beyond with people and organizations in all three sectors around the world.

√ Leading beyond the walls of the enterprise and building the organization's share of the healthy, cohesive community. Forming partnerships, alliances, and collaborations that spell synergy, success, and significance.

This checklist for viability is only a beginning. Changing circumstances will require additions as new challenges arise, and deletions where needs have been met. New customers must be welcomed as we move beyond the old walls both physically and psychologically.

Tomorrow may be tenuous for the leader and organization of the future, but the message is clear and powerful: Managing for mission, innovation, and diversity will sustain us and those we serve on the long journey to 2010.

[2001]

PART III

Leading in a New Century, a New World

LEADING in a new century means leading in a new world. September 11, 2001, was the day that caused leaders in all three sectors to mark the day of heroism and grieving, the day when leaders knew they were leading in a different world. That September day changed the old assumptions and expectations, and brought new dimensions and new ambiguities to the lives of leaders in all three sectors. Leading in a society that has changed forever, leaders are asking if this altered world means changing why we lead and how we lead—and if we must change our basic values and principles, the "how to be" of our leadership.

Leaders in all three sectors, public, private, and social—government, business, and nonprofit—are finding that some of the how to's, the ways, the circumstances are changing as the world outside changes. Yet the mission—why we do what we do, the values and principles that are the basis of all strategy—is essential, enduring. Mission, values, customer focus, and being customer- and demographics-driven do not change in these times of massive change and global turbulence. Out of the testing, the crucible, these fundamentals endure. Leadership is a matter of how to be, not how to do it. In the end it is the quality and character of the leader that determine the performance, the results. Mission is the guiding star, why we do what we do. Our values hold, permeate, bring certainty in uncertain times. And if ever being demographics-driven was a powerful measurement of viability, the time is now to describe the organization of the future for leaders of the future as mission-focused, values-based, and demographics-driven. These chapters focus on leadership in a changing world even as the leaders who read these pages are shaping that world. Leaders are the embodiment of the mission, values, beliefs, and principles that are the soul of the organization.

CHAPTER 14

A World of Ideas

A NEW WAVE of globalization is transforming nations and organizations. It has little to do with the market economy or industrial expansion; it has everything to do with leadership and management ideas that are sweeping the intellectual landscape.

The sea change is evident in the experience of the Drucker Foundation itself. The Foundation began with a simple challenge: how to share wisdom on leadership and management with the leaders of nonprofit social sector organizations. It was thought we would be addressing the leaders of U.S. organizations, but it soon became clear that the issues of managing for the mission and building more responsive, inclusive institutions had worldwide relevance and appeal.

Since our first overseas seminar, in 1992, our experience has confirmed that discovery. The three volumes of our Future Series—*The Leader of the Future, The Organization of the Future,* and *The Community of the Future*—have been translated into sixteen languages, with more than three hundred thousand copies in print worldwide, and now eight more books, five instructional tools, a journal, and many conferences deliver the messages around the world. Over the past years, I have had the remarkable opportunity to speak in a dozen countries, from the established democracies of Scandinavia to the emerging markets of Eastern Europe, China and other fast-growing Asian economies, and the revitalized societies of Latin America. Regardless of the specific subject at hand, the backdrop in every setting was the same: building the viable, relevant organization of the future in a time of massive societal change.

From these visits, we have gained a renewed belief in two enduring truths: first, healthy societies are built on equally vibrant public, private, and nonprofit sectors. Second, the leaders of these three sectors must achieve results in their organizations while looking, working, and leading beyond the walls of their own enterprises.

From countries as different as Peru, Poland, and the Philippines we have found effective leaders to share certain characteristics:

Hesselbein on Leadership

- Determination to be a viable and relevant part of the tenuous future

- Belief in the essential role of mission for inspiration, direction, and mobilization

- Practice of innovation throughout the enterprise

- Rejection of hierarchy in favor of flexible, inclusive management systems

- Openness to new models, new ideas, and new initiatives regardless of where in the world they come from

- A common language, no matter what tongue is spoken, that embraces the basic concepts of principled leadership

- Belief that the social sector must be the essential and equal partner of business and government

- Willingness to move beyond the walls (of organizations and sectors) and join in the emerging partnerships that are essential to building the healthy society

When the remarkable political and economic changes began in the nations of Eastern Europe in the '80s and '90s, many believed that the driving forces of the renewed society would be democratic governments and free market economies.

Experience has shown that a vital social sector of community organizations is necessary as well.

While the Drucker Foundation was presenting a seminar to more than eight hundred participants in Argentina, Father Rafael Braun, a distinguished social sector leader and a founder of *Fundación Compromiso,* said of his country: "After fifty years of social disintegration, at last we have a chance to build a social sector, for without it, we cannot sustain the democracy." He captured the truth we have seen demonstrated again and again: a vital civil society is built upon the three legs of government, business, and nonprofit organizations.

When the Drucker Foundation delivers a seminar abroad, the four or five consultants, business leaders, or authors who present the sessions go as volunteers. Invariably we learn as much or more from our hosts as they do from us. Often these lessons take the form of a memorable, emotional moment.

On a November day in Lima, it was very moving to work with three hundred businessmen on a remarkable vision of the future. Their organization, Peru 2021, has developed a comprehensive vision of their country in 2021, the 200th anniversary of Peru's revolution. Their vision encompasses the economy, education, environment, and technology of the next century. These leaders' genuine interest in defining corporate social responsibility and building cross-sector partnerships showed that what we sometimes regard as domestic goals are in fact universal aspirations.

Leaders everywhere affirm our saying that everything begins with mission, that the mission statement should be short, powerful, and compelling, and that, as Peter Drucker says, it should fit on a T-shirt. While working in Geneva with the staff of the International Federation of the Red Cross and Red Crescent Societies, I said that I use their mission—"To serve the most vulnerable"—as the best example of what we preach. They responded by presenting me with a T-shirt with the Drucker Foundation's mission on the front (yes, it does fit: "To lead social sector organizations toward excellence in performance") and our three Future Series books on the back. Mission is playing a new and powerful role in the emerging social sectors around the world, even as the power of mission is being rediscovered in established civil societies.

Wherever I go, Peter Drucker's definition of *innovation*—change that creates a new dimension of performance—hits home. Innovation is an indispensable part of moving into the future, and it occurs mostly through collaboration. Yet not all leaders of governments and businesses see social sector organizations, whether long-established or newly emerging, as an essential partner of the public and private sectors. It is with these leaders that we must convey not only the size and significance of their country's own voluntary social sector but the global significance: there are twenty million social sector organizations worldwide; only 5 percent of these are adequately funded, yet together they generate annual revenues of one trillion American dollars.

Drucker's sober statement, "It is not government, it is not

business, it is the social sector that may yet save the society," helps place in perspective the significance of the third sector worldwide.

The spread of ideas does not require that we travel. The Internet moves ideas around the world, e-mail arrives with sometimes disconcerting speed, and the ubiquitous fax connects us with people and ideas twenty-four hours a day. And the Drucker Foundation can reach ten thousand leaders in five countries through a seminar by satellite.

The Drucker Foundation e-mail—Innovation of the Week—presents an example of an outstanding nonprofit program or project, real-life models of innovation—models that work, that can be adopted, or that just excite the imagination of friends across town or ten thousand miles away. The Los Angeles homeless service organization Chrysalis, for example, stimulates innovation with its mission, "Changing lives through jobs."

In Manila, where we visited Father Rocky Evangelista's center for street children, our team knew that we had found there a model of innovation that could travel around the world, that could "make success travel." Later, as our team spoke to students, faculty, and business leaders at the Asian Institute of Management (the distinguished graduate school), the dialogue was so spirited and the connection so strong that we were reluctant to leave. On our last day in Manila, a rally of four hundred teenagers—Girl Scouts, choirs, school classes, and their leaders—honored us. In a discussion with these young leaders we were impressed with the quality of the questions and the poise of the students. One fifteen-year-old wrote later that she'll always remember "Walk like you talk."

The common ties mark every encounter. In Warsaw, our team of American business, civic, and nonprofit leaders arrived the week the new Polish Constitution was inaugurated. Remembering that the Polish Revolution followed the American Revolution of 1776, we shared a moment of high significance with our Polish colleagues.

There is a miraculous openness today. The barriers are down; we are learning from one another in a wondrously circular exchange. In the global social sector there is a sense of urgency, a sense that perhaps at this moment in history we have a rare opportunity—the three sectors together—to create a new kind of world that is linked by ideas. And this can be the real legacy of globalization: changed lives and cohesive communities.

[1998]

CHAPTER 15

Speaking
a Common
Language

TODAY, leaders speak a common language. Across the three sectors—business, government, and nonprofit sectors—and around the world, we speak this common language.

The language of leadership and management—where mission and vision, goals and strategy, travel easily from east to west—and managing for the mission have the same power, wherever there are leaders who hold before their people the mission—why they do what they do—their reason for being, the purpose of the organization.

Today, for business, government, and nonprofit leaders of change, the principles of leadership and management are basic; they are fundamental; they are generic to all organizations in all three sectors, and they are global—as true in Beijing as in Boston.

That is the message I delivered in October 2000 in a series of seminars in China. At the invitation of the Bright China Management Institute, a team of four thought leaders with the Drucker Foundation met with more than two thousand business, government, and emerging social sector leaders. For seven days in three cities we talked about managing for the mission—the need for leaders to hold before their people why they do what they do, their reason for being.

As we talked with our Chinese colleagues, we used the same language to describe the power of mission that we use when we work with the Salvation Army, the U.S. Army, Texaco, or the American Federation of Arts. *Vision. Mission. Goals.* The actual words are different in every language, but the meaning of those words is universal. And with a common language, people in every sector, in every culture, can have dialogues of great meaning. This has not always been the case.

Twelve years ago, when the Drucker Foundation was founded, some in the social sector questioned whether *customer* could be used to describe their clients, patients, service recipients, or members. But slowly the word became part of a management vocabulary that enabled social sector leaders to communicate without translation.

It was clear that common characteristics demanded common terms—a common glossary. The powerful management books by Peter F. Drucker, Charles Handy, Peter Senge, Regina

Herzlinger, and James Austin spoke to no single sector—they belonged to all three. Jim Collins and Jerry Porras's *Built to Last* made as much sense to the Girl Scouts as to General Motors—this at the same time that *Be, Know, Do,* the Army leadership field manual, is as relevant to a newly commissioned lieutenant, a noncommissioned officer, or a civilian employee as to a colonel.

Throughout the three sectors, a marvelous sense of inclusion and collaboration permeates our organizations, our enterprises. Our common leadership language unleashes new alliances, new partnerships, new understanding as organizations in all three sectors move beyond the walls of the old and toward a new realization of the common good.

For instance, Investment in America, a forum of The Conference Board, the U.S. Army, and the Drucker Foundation, supports the Army's Partnership for Youth Success, through which two hundred corporations promise good jobs to young men and women when they complete their military service. No need for translation in this partnership. And the Texaco Management Institute delivers world-class management training to leaders of advocacy and other nonprofit groups. For them, managing for the mission, for innovation, for diversity resonates in both the corporation and the community.

The rapid proliferation of college and university nonprofit management programs and centers is also building a common vocabulary for change, partnership, and community. In 1998, there were 180 colleges and universities with courses in nonprofit management, up from just 17 in 1990. Here again, listening to the customer has become the common focus—the common language.

Demographics-driven is as relevant to a college as to an e-commerce start-up, and innovation is a universal imperative. When we cling to our insider vocabulary, we end up talking to ourselves. Today even *marketing*—once a suspect word in some corners of the public and nonprofit sectors—has become an essential discipline, with a common understanding that it is about serving the needs of customers.

The nuances of the new language allow for true dialogue. No longer do we settle for the didactic pronouncement, "Nonprofits have to be managed like businesses." Today we respond, "No, nonprofits must manage in a businesslike way." Similar words, different meanings, new understanding.

Values-based is as essential for the American Red Cross as for American Express. At one time there was little movement across the sectors—corporate executives climbed the corporate ladder; nonprofit executives moved, perhaps, to other nonprofits; and government leaders found their way to and from the other sectors. Today there is a flow of corporate and government executives to nonprofit leadership roles. Each move underscores the fluidity of leadership among all sectors, and each leader speaks the more inclusive, nonhierarchical language of the future. There is no up-down, top-bottom, superior-subordinate language for the newly mobile, newly agile, emerging leadership corps. These leaders are as at ease in the boardroom as in the classroom.

I travel frequently, spending one-third of my time with corporations, one-third with social sector nonprofits, and one-third with colleges and universities. As I travel from Australia to Denmark to Mexico to China to Peru to Poland—and in the United States—wherever I find an airport and an audience I use the same philosophy and language. Both are fundamental and generic. The examples and applications may change, but the message is circular and universal.

There is wonderment in the ease with which our leaders transcend the old barriers, breach the old walls, and share a new appreciation of the differences that can enrich our lives. For such leaders, language is more than a tool, a skill, or a simple vehicle for communication. It is the thread that binds us together, creates new understanding, leads us to new action, and then strengthens and builds communities. It is men and women speaking the language of inclusion, appreciation, and wholeness who sustain the democracy.

[2001]

CHAPTER 16

Seeing Your
Contribution
Life Size

A S PETER DRUCKER has written, "The more economy, money, and information become global, the more *community* will matter. And only the social sector nonprofit organization performs in the community, exploits its opportunities, mobilizes its local resources, solves its problems. The social sector nonprofit organization will thus largely determine the values, the vision, the cohesion, and the performance of the 21st century society."

The social sector encompasses 1.5 million nonprofit organizations in the United States and 20 million around the world. These organizations generate a trillion dollars a year and, more important, they share a common bottom line—changed lives.

Yet members of voluntary organizations often fail to see themselves life size. As board members, officers, staff, or volunteers, we too often think of ourselves as junior partners of business and government. And to understate the value of our contributions, whatever our position in the enterprise, is dangerous to the future of nonprofit organizations and their growing significance.

There are many reasons for this outdated self-image. As a society we often have undervalued the volunteer position, perhaps because it did not carry a salary with it. Some saw the management of nonprofits as somehow softer, their executives as less professional.

Lessons from Nonprofits

In recent years that view has begun to change. Peter Drucker has long counseled corporate leaders to look to nonprofits for lessons in managing for the mission, making the most of the board, allocating scant resources, and attracting and managing the workforce. Increasingly, corporations and government agencies see the social sector as a training ground for their emerging leaders. Hewlett-Packard, Texaco, Ford, General Electric, and others show a new appreciation for teamwork, commitment, and service that come of community involvement.

New forms of partnerships now link organizations across all sectors of the economy. With these partnerships comes a growing recognition that we must deal with challenges, as the Army puts it, "on the ground," where people live (and where community-based organizations thrive). We see, too, that many government programs have not reached people as was hoped, and that no sector can solve society's problems alone.

In short, we are seeing that the benefits of business, government, and social sector collaboration are circular. Not only are we changing the lives of people but in the process are changing the partner organizations themselves. That makes the contributions of volunteer organizations even greater.

Today part of every leader's job, whether in business, government, or the social sector, is to help people see the full value of what they contribute. That starts by using more inclusive language—eliminating from our vocabulary "subordinate" and "superior" and talking instead about colleagues, members, and partners. How we talk about people's contributions, deploy their talents at work, and structure the organization, has everything to do with how people perform. "I am just a volunteer" or "I am a cog in the wheel" does not build a vibrant and engaged organization.

Satisfaction Beyond Salary

In a society that sometimes seems to value wealth above all, the most effective leaders in many businesses are seeking greater significance, a satisfaction beyond the salary. They find that social sector organizations provide new kinds of opportunities to others and themselves. To meet these new expectations, non-profits must first measure results. We don't judge nonprofits by their good intentions; we assess their performance and results.

Some nonprofits have found it difficult to measure the common bottom line—changed lives—but are learning that it is not only possible but necessary to do so. If we plan well, at the beginning of the year we can set goals and specific, measurable objectives that further the mission. At the end of the year we can then assess our performance against our goals and objectives. Organizational self-assessment is a powerful tool, and can help every member of the enterprise appreciate his or her contribution.

When we recruit volunteers to serve in a nonprofit organization, we begin with a clearly defined job description. If I am a volunteer, I know exactly what is expected of me. I know that I have staff partners and continuing training to support me in the job and that at the end of the year we will evaluate personal and organizational performance. Without a disciplined and respectful approach to recruitment, orientation, support, assessment, and recognition, we will have lower performance and a disenchanted volunteer.

Recognition is critical. We must regularly acknowledge the contributions of those within and outside the organization. We give volunteers, staff, and donors respect, recognition, and continuing opportunities. In every way we communicate, we reinforce the indispensable nature of their service.

Many corporations commit to a human, social, or environmental bottom line as well as a financial one. This commitment can be more motivating than financial objectives alone. It adds power to a compelling mission. The job of bringing a mission to life—and making others own it—falls squarely upon the leader. When we talk to our people, we share mission, goals, objectives, and results so everyone can see the outward evidence of the inward motivation. That is what builds a sense of significance and accomplishment throughout the organization.

The most effective social sector organizations have moved from expecting to have their good intentions rewarded to holding themselves accountable for results. So too they must move from seeing themselves as junior members to knowing they are equal partners of business and government. It is only through equal membership in these new partnerships across sectors that we can build the healthy, inclusive society our people deserve.

[2000]

CHAPTER 17

When They Look at Us, Can They Find Themselves?

O UR GREATEST thought leaders use elegant, spare language to challenge tomorrow's leaders and organizations. In 1980, in *Managing in Turbulent Times*, Peter Drucker wrote: "A time of turbulence is a dangerous time, but its greatest danger is a temptation to deny reality." In 1989, in *Leadership Is an Art*, Max De Pree wrote: "The first responsibility of a leader is to define reality."

Resisting the temptation to deny reality and daring to define the new realities may be a leader's greatest challenges. The challenges we confront today are numerous and daunting, but perhaps the most pressing are the demographic shifts that are reshaping Western society. Given the growing impact of these changes on our society and its institutions, our ability to see the remarkable opportunities in the growing diversity—not try to "manage" it—may decide the future of our organizations.

How we help people deal with their deepest differences is not just a challenge for public officials; far from it. Every leader, in the smallest community agency or the largest corporation, needs to anticipate the effects of rapid demographic change on the people, the services, and the resources of every market and community. For example, by 2025 the Asian American population will have more than doubled to 7.5 percent of the population from just over 3 percent in 1995, according to U.S. Census Bureau estimates (see Figure 17.1). The Hispanic population will grow to nearly 17 percent from 10 percent, African Americans will increase to 14 percent from 12 percent, and in the same period the white population will shrink to 62 percent from 74 percent.

If we fail on the key challenge of equal access to opportunity, our efforts in every other area may falter. It does little good to formulate a brilliant competitive strategy unless we include the people inside the organization who must carry it out and the people in the marketplace and the community who will benefit. To further our mission and build the richly diverse organization, we must make inclusion and participation top priorities for all governance and management teams. "Mission-focused," "values-based," and "demographics-driven" will describe the viable and relevant organization of the future.

Figure 17.1 The Changing Face of America

Projected Population Distribution

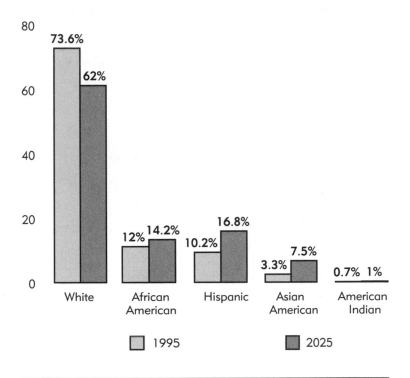

Source: U.S. Census Bureau

When They Look at Us

Understanding Diversity

The language we use as leaders will determine whether the people of the enterprise see demographic change as a threat to the organization's present status, or as a remarkable opportunity to innovate. Making our organization demographics-driven can be a catalyst for change, a way to build a more productive workforce, find new significance and new ways to serve, and build a more cohesive community.

We cannot ensure equal access or build upon our diverse strengths by sitting at our desks and proclaiming, "Let there be diversity." Rather, we must scan the environment and gather current and credible information about our workforce, our boards, our supporters, our customers, and our communities. Understanding our constituents' demographics is key to meeting their needs, and to creating conditions in which the diversity of the organization brings new vitality to the workplace and to our neighborhoods.

Only with such understanding can our leadership teams hold before the people of the organization a vision of the future. For our most effective organizations, that vision will include a richly diverse organization with governance, management, and the workforce representative of the whole community. Leaders of these organizations know it takes committed, energetic, and able people to serve present and future customers who are the changing community.

Steps Toward the Future

If the vision is inspiring, the mission is compelling, and the goal of equal access is unambiguous—and all three are clearly communicated throughout the organization—what are the essential steps toward building the vibrant, viable, relevant, and productive enterprise?

I have found that defining the reality of equal access is a five-part process:

1. A vision of a diverse future—with rich representation throughout the organization, starting with the board and management team—begins and remains a clear priority of the leader. That vision must be shared across the organization and among leaders at every level, but the board chairman and chief executive retain the final responsibility for achieving equal access.

2. The annual plan of work and its supporting budget include specific action steps and activities that ensure the realization of the vision.

3. All policies, practices, and procedures are examined for barriers to full board, management, and workforce participation. We abandon policies that impede, while developing policies that facilitate inclusion.

4. We ask the board, the management team, the dispersed leadership of the organization, the sales force,

and the workforce all to consider one shared question: "When our potential customers look at us, can they find themselves?" This key question is as important for our marketing and educational materials—print and electronic—as it is for our people.

5. If the answers (to "Can they find themselves?") are not what we want them to be, we mobilize around the shared vision and together define how we will get there. Here again, language is important. We purge our vocabulary of the tired language of "managing diversity" and use the powerful and positive language of future relevance and viability—of equal access.

Building Commitment and Accountability

In assessing our performance we look not just at people currently employed and engaged, we examine those still making their way into our orbit, as prospective leaders, customers, donors, contributors, or partners. Are we grooming people today for tomorrow's leadership positions? Are there new faces in the pipeline? And in the position descriptions of all those who direct the work of others, is there a clearly stated accountability for building the richly diverse organization we require?

Our customers of tomorrow will be far more diverse than those we are serving today; so in addition to using demographics as an indispensable planning tool, we also study the psychographics of our new constituents—how they think and feel—what they value.

The challenges of leadership and citizenship are daunting, yet they offer incredible opportunities for new significance and performance if we have the courage and commitment to define the new realities in human terms. In doing so we free up the organization, release the spirits of our people, embrace the changes in workplace and workforce, and open doors by providing equal access to opportunity supported by development, education, and commitment for full and energetic participation.

Turbulent times create possibilities beyond today's most optimistic views. Leaders can unleash the talents and energies of all their people as they pursue a vision of a country of healthy children, strong families, decent housing, good schools, and work that dignifies, all embraced by the inclusive, cohesive community. We have a long way to go before we fully appreciate, let alone redefine, current realities. But the individual efforts of thousands of leaders in millions of organizations will transform the vision into the new reality. When they look at us, they *will* find themselves.

[1999]

CHAPTER 18

A Call to Leaders

THERE IS great anxiety about the future of our children. There is an equally strong sense of urgency. The anxiety has many faces, and we can distill it into one burning question: "What can we do, now, to provide a healthy, supportive community for today's children—not for tomorrow's children, but for today's?" It is a question that leaders in all our organizations must answer.

Recently the violence that flares daily in our streets—and occasionally in our workplaces—has spilled into a church in Fort Worth, Texas; into a community center in Los Angeles; and into school yards in Colorado, Georgia, Oregon, Arkansas, Kentucky, and Mississippi. Headlines, TV images, editorials, and countless panels and speeches illuminate no clear cause, direction, or focus—only fragmented opinions and response.

These random horrors are only the most recent examples of the risks facing today's young people. The forces threatening our children's well-being are tremendous. But so are the resources available for helping children: the potential energy and commitment of leaders—men and women in public, private, and social sector organizations embracing a specific initiative that can touch a young person, improve a school class, enrich a community group.

Making a Difference Today

Social sector organizations are mobilizing thousands of organizations and millions of volunteers to bring hope to children who otherwise might see little in their future. Youth organizations across the country such as the Girl Scouts, the Boy Scouts, Big Brothers Big Sisters, YMCA, YWCA, 4-H, Boys & Girls Clubs of America, Girls Inc., Junior Achievement, and many others have accelerated their individual and collective efforts—reaching millions of children, youths, and their families in local communities. Colleges, universities, and communities of faith are part of the solution as well.

Yet despite all the individual and organizational effort, the needs are accelerating, the problems deepening. The house is on fire.

What could happen if leaders in all three sectors acknowledge that what we are doing is not enough, that much more must be done now? What if every company, small and large, sought out a nonprofit organization with which to partner—addressing a critical need of children and young people in its community? The people of the corporation and the people of a nonprofit working together on a critical issue could change the lives of today's young people.

We might look as well to military bases all over the country, where remarkable role models—servicemen and women—could volunteer to give young people a close-up view of principled, disciplined, concerned, and generous leaders whose commitment to their country includes a commitment to its children.

Looking Beyond the Walls

In the pages of *Leader to Leader* and on our Drucker Foundation Web site, you can read about "beyond the walls." The Drucker Foundation's book *Leading Beyond the Walls* and *Meeting the Collaboration Challenge* workbook and videotape describe the kind of innovative action and partnerships that will help define our future. Look out your office window. With too many of our schools in disarray, children falling far short of their own potential, some classrooms lacking adequate supplies, books, and teacher support, there are many ways to help. For two years I have been Principal for a Day at the New School for Arts and Science in the South Bronx. Last year the school had no library. This year it does.

Countless groups and individuals around the country have adopted a school, supported a class, brought young people together around an idea or project, and given service to a community effort. Some colleges have seen this as an opportunity for their students to serve as mentors—giving their time and energy back to the community by reaching out to children in need. Corporations have given the time and service of employees to contribute their energy, expertise, and example. Such efforts strengthen the character, the will, the hope of the young—and enrich the lives of their elders. If finding the opportunity, young person, group, or issue seems difficult, local Volunteer Centers and United Ways are a telephone call or Internet visit away. Our Drucker Nonprofit Innovation Discovery Site (www.pfdf.org/innovation/index.html), with its e-mail Innovation of the Week, is filled with examples of community partnerships at work.

Leading beyond the walls of one's organization, industry, and sector can bring new meaning to our everyday work and important results to our communities. Children can't wait for solutions that might take a generation to work. Today is theirs and ours.

You may ask why I am issuing this call in a leadership book. But what better place? Only with inspired leadership will we break the psychological barriers that inhibit us from moving into uncharted and perhaps uncomfortable waters. Provid-

Hesselbein on Leadership

ing equal access to opportunity is a formidable challenge. Leaders can make the personal and organizational commitments that mobilize others. Sometimes just listening is the greatest gift. But reaching out in a tangible way is key. The walls of our organizations were built up over many years. To change lives we need to move beyond the walls and reach out to the community today. Later will be too late for a generation of kids.

A Society That Cares Not

In 1981, when I first met Peter Drucker, I heard him say, "We live in a society that pretends to care about its children, but it does not." That day, I tried to think of a way to refute his statement, but I could not. Two decades later, society is even more fragmented in providing the healthy environment all its young people deserve. Recent tragedies have awakened us. Yet to make a difference we need a community-by-community mobilization of focus, will, energy, and commitment. Perhaps this is the moment when, child by child, adult by adult, we all move into a new era of leadership, service, and commitment to children.

The U.S. Army says, "Our soldiers are our credentials." As a society, can we say of our schools, "Our students are our credentials"? We will be measured by how we respond to today's urgent call. The young cannot speak for themselves; their actions, their anxiety, turmoil, and here-and-now needs speak for them. As leaders, how will we respond?

[2000]

CHAPTER 19

The Dream That Lies Before Us

THE VIABLE COMMUNITY—one that embraces healthy children, strong families, good schools, decent housing, and work that dignifies, all in the cohesive, inclusive society that cares about all of its people—is a dream that lies before us.

Against the realities of our times, it is clear that the dream will remain a dream until we move beyond the barriers we have built, consciously or unconsciously, around race, gender, equal access, and the composition of the workforce. The old answers do not fit the new questions and challenges, so all of us who care about building and renewing community must begin with the premise that this is the biggest job in town and no one sector, no one government, no one industry, can mobilize citizens—men and women and the young—to create the new community, the inclusive community that embraces all its people. The day of partnership is upon us, and these new partnerships can become the engine that drives the renewal of community.

Piecemeal, tentative efforts to address only symptoms of critical community need will not work. Incisive analysis, identification of needs, and a powerful plan for the deployment of people and the allocation of resources to address those needs, with measurable results, are required.

If ever great corporate leaders needed to move beyond the walls to lead the ultimate effort, it is now. Religious leaders, university and college presidents, and the leaders of voluntary organizations need to add their vision and voices to the leadership effort. If ever the team approach—the building of community described in human terms—was needed, it is here. Inclusive teams for every aspect of the initiative are essential to success. When the people of the community to be served observe these teams at work, they can find themselves.

To mobilize the whole community, these leaders will lead by voice and example. They will hold the dream before the people. Those they hope to serve will see themselves, not just as beneficiaries, but as partners in the common task. Managing the dream becomes part of the reality.

In today's community we find high anxiety over the scope and magnitude of the challenge. Peter Drucker, in the opening of *The Community of the Future,* describes the historical context and immense significance of the task of "civilizing the cities." How do we begin?

First, we find leaders who believe that the community is as much their business as is the business of their enterprise. They dedicate the same commitment to this job, the same forecasting, planning, marketing, and mobilization of energy and initiative, that they dedicate to building the enterprise within the walls. These men and women—leaders in all three sectors—exist in every community. We need only a handful of leaders, with a vision of what their community could be, to drive the effort. They involve the public, private, and social sectors as they plan the campaign for the renewed community. The mobilization has to be as inclusive as the community we envision.

This sturdy band of leaders will build on existing strengths. What are the strengths of the community? If schools are good and housing poor, the priority is clear. If children are at risk in any way—health, safety, caring environments, family support—the solutions are built upon the existing strengths. If all three sectors are working only within their own walls, these leaders inspire others to move beyond the walls to build new cross-sector partnerships for a brighter future. Goals will be communicated in powerful and compelling statements throughout the community until there is a pervasive sense of ownership.

The new partnerships—a government agency with a nonprofit organization, a nonprofit organization with a corporation, sometimes all three together—each with a clearly stated share of the project and with measurable goals, are part of the community's own plan for its renewal and rebuilding. But some people have to care enough to dare to take the lead. These will be the real heroes of the future—the men and women who decide the time is now—and their leadership moment for the greater good is now.

The litany of community needs in many cities is long and daunting, but measured against what the future could be, leaders will find a balance of challenge and opportunity. The new partners will search for initiatives that are successful and will move ahead, sharing examples and models. Here and there, all over this country, are successful, real-life examples of community partnerships that are changing lives and building community. Leaders will "help success travel" and share the stories widely.

In New York City's Washington Heights neighborhood, the port of entry for immigrants from the Dominican Republic and the site of extended police and neighborhood confrontation in the early 1990s, the Children's Aid Society has developed a remarkable partnership. Working with the public school system of New York, Children's Aid has established five community schools. Public elementary and middle schools, the community schools combine the public school system with a remarkable partnership of more than seventy private non-profit organizations. At I.S. 218, for example, students receive health services from the Visiting Nurse Association, participate in after-school activities from Outward Bound, and can work in the "Recycle-a-Bicycle" room run by Transportation Alternatives. The school is open from 7:00 A.M. to 10:00 P.M. six days a week and offers courses to adults in the evening in addition to after-school activities for the children. After five years of operation, the community schools have become the centers of a renewed community in Washington Heights.

Also in New York City, but on the Lower East Side, the Henry Street Settlement runs an annual partnership program with managers from United Parcel Service. Since 1968, UPS has sent fourteen managers to serve as community interns with Henry Street. The program lasts a month and is not a voluntary commitment, but rather an important part of the UPS executive development process. The managers assigned to the internship provide professional services to the Henry Street Settlement. In exchange, Henry Street shows the managers how it works with families and individuals who are facing the challenges of unemployment, drug use, violence, and poverty. The managers benefit from the chance to see both the challenges and successes of Henry Street's work. They return to their own communities with a heightened awareness of the diversity and depth of the challenges we all face. Their lives are changed. The program is a vivid example of the mutual benefits derived from those serving and those being served.

At the Drucker Foundation's 1996 leadership and management conference, "Beyond the Walls: Partnerships for a Better Future," Hewlett-Packard Company was the Foundation's partner. This was not a case of "they write check, we do work," but rather a collaborative example of high involvement from both HP and the Foundation. HP executives worked as a team with the Drucker Foundation staff, volunteering, coordinating speaker sessions, and providing the technology and speaker support. This partnership, initiated by HP, made a highly visible and significant impact on an important conference on innovation and partnership.

In Connecticut, the Eviction Prevention Program—a partnership between the nonprofit organization Community Mediation and the state's Department of Social Services—has prevented hundreds of evictions and saved the state millions of dollars. By combining CM's ability to bring tenants and landlords together in mutual negotiation and state funds to cover back rent and mortgage payments, this partnership keeps families together and at home. In addition, the state saves significantly; the cost of providing rent and mortgage to prevent evictions is far less than the cost of providing homeless services.

These community partnerships can serve as models and inspirations for us all. Building the healthy, inclusive community begins with building a healthy human enterprise, with teams working across the organization and a high involvement of people in decisions that affect them, providing learning and teaching opportunities for everyone. Because everything begins with mission, the mission will emerge as the essential part of building the enterprise of the future. Mission can mobilize the people of the organization around why they do what they do, and it gives purpose to what they do and how they do it, just as the mission of renewing community can inspire and mobilize the total community effort.

It is not only the social, nonprofit sector that shares a common bottom line, changing lives. All three sectors are indispensable as they join forces and build and renew the community—the community of the future our children require and deserve.

Moving beyond the walls—in powerful partnerships that can build and heal and unify—leaders are called to manage the dream of a country of healthy children, strong families, good schools, decent housing, and work that dignifies, all embraced by the cohesive, inclusive community. It is the dream that lies before us.

[1998]

THE AUTHOR

FRANCES HESSELBEIN is the chairman of the board of governors of the Peter F. Drucker Foundation for Non-profit Management, and served as its founding president and chief executive officer from 1990 to 2000. An international speaker and seminar leader on leadership and management excellence, she has presented sessions for leaders of organizations from all three sectors, including ServiceMaster, National Urban League, KidsPeace, the U.S. Army, Chevron, Texaco, Lutheran Social Services, Eastman Kodak, Hewlett-Packard, the World Bank, Business for Social Responsibility, California Highway Patrol, the U.S. Naval Academy, and the U.S. Coast Guard. She chaired a Salzburg seminar on managing nongovernmental organizations for leaders from Eastern and

Western Europe, Asia, Africa, and Latin America that was cosponsored by the W. K. Kellogg and Drucker Foundations. She has spoken at conferences in Austria, Canada, Denmark, England, India, Iran, Mexico, the Netherlands, Pakistan, Peru, Austria, and Switzerland, and has led Drucker Foundation teams to Argentina, Australia, China, the Philippines, and Poland to present leadership and management seminars.

She serves on numerous nonprofit and private sector corporate boards, including those of the Mutual of America Life Insurance Company, Harvard Business School's Initiative for Social Enterprise, the Hauser Center for Nonprofit Organizations at Harvard, Points of Light Foundation, Volunteers of America, and the advisory board of the Broad Foundation's Center for School Superintendents.

Editor in chief of the quarterly leadership and management journal *Leader to Leader,* she is coeditor of the book of the same name, as well as the three volumes of the Drucker Foundation Future Series, *The Community of the Future, The Organization of the Future*, and the best-selling *The Leader of the Future,* which has been translated into sixteen languages. Other books she has coedited are *Leading Beyond the Walls, Leading for Innovation*, and the four Leader to Leader Guides, *On Mission and Leadership, On Leading Change, On High-Performance Organizations*, and *On Creativity, Innovation, and Renewal.*

Hesselbein was awarded the Presidential Medal of Freedom, the United States of America's highest civilian honor, in January 1998. The award recognized her leadership as chief executive officer of Girl Scouts of the USA from 1976 to 1990, as well as her role as founding president of the Peter F. Drucker Foundation for Nonprofit Management. Her contributions were also recognized by former President Bush, who appointed her to two presidential commissions on community service, the board of directors of the Commission on National and Community Service in August 1991, and his advisory committee on the Points of Light Initiative Foundation in 1989. In February 1999, Hesselbein was awarded the Legion of Honor Gold Medallion from the Chapel of the Four Chaplains, the Distinguished Alumni Fellows Award from the University of Pittsburgh, and in 2001, the International ATHENA Award. In 2001 she was awarded the Henry A. Rosso Medal for Lifetime Achievement in Ethical Fund Raising from Indiana University's Center on Philanthropy.

The recipient of sixteen honorary doctoral degrees, Hesselbein has given commencement addresses and lectures at numerous colleges and universities, including Arizona State, Boston College, Fordham, Harvard Business School, Pennsylvania State College, Princeton Theological Seminary, Stanford, University of Michigan, University of Nebraska at Kearny, University of Pittsburgh, University of Richmond, Thiel College, University of St. Thomas, and Yale School of Management. Harvard Business School has published a case study of her work with Girl Scouts of the USA.

She has been featured on the covers of *BusinessWeek* and *Savvy* magazines as an example of managerial excellence, as well as in issues of *Fortune* and *Chief Executive* as an exemplary leader. Hesselbein appears in the management videotape *The Leader Within* with Warren Bennis, and moderates or is featured in a number of The Nonprofit Drucker Series of management audiotapes. She was the first woman to be inducted into the Johnstown Pennsylvania Business Hall of Fame and was awarded the Distinguished Citizen of the Commonwealth by the Pennsylvania Society, and Distinguished Daughter of Pennsylvania by the governor. She is included in *Who's Who in America, Who's Who in Finance and Industry,* and *Who's Who in the World.*

INDEX

F

Finances: focusing and allocating, 88, 89; saving state service costs, 136

Focus: and allocating finances, 88, 89; on mission, 9, 22–23, 86, 106; on task not gender, 26–29. *See also* Mission, the

Future Series books (Drucker Foundation), 98, 101

Future, the, 49; checklist for viability in, 86–90; five questions for, 81–82; leadership transition for, 41–46; population diversity in, 117–124

G

Galvin, Bob, 61

Gender, and organizational leadership, 25–29

Generosity, 38

Gettysburg, the battle of, 82

Gilmore, Thomas North, 43

Girl Scouts of the USA, xiii–xvii, 3, 43, 141

Glossary, common. *See* Language

Goals: organization, 38, 86, 114; personal, 74–75

Good Samaritan, the, 59

Governance and management, 90

Government sector: partnerships, 134–136; U.S. Army, 80, 82, 107; U.S. Census Bureau, 118, 119. *See also* Schools

H

Harvard Business School, 80–81

Henry Street Settlement (New York City), 135

Herman Miller company, 68

Heroes, 4, 16–17

Hesselbein, Frances, 139–142; board memberships of, 140; conferences participation by, 3, 80, 140; editing and publications by, 140; leadership positions held by, xiii–xvii, 3, 139; recognition and awards to, 140–142; seminar leadership by, 139–140; speaking activities of, 98, 109, 139. *See also* Peter F. Drucker Foundation for Nonprofit Management

Hewlett-Packard Company, 15; partnerships conference, 135–136

Hierarchies: past pyramid, 51–52; rejection of, 67–68, 99. *See also* Circular management systems

Leaders (*cont.*)
14–16; the question of developing, 77–79, 112, 135; transition of, 41–46, 88; women, 26–29

Leadership: the author's definition of, 3; barriers to (two types), 37–40; civility a tool of, 32; distributing, 8–9, 33, 68–69, 89; fluidity among sectors, 108–109; from the front, 69, 89; gender and organizational, 25–29; "how to be," 3–4, 7–11, 21, 69, 95–96; learning, 61–62, 79–81, 135; preparation questions, 72–73; societal significance of, 9–10; transition and succession, 41–46, 88; values-driven, 14–16

Learning: continuing, 87; to lead, 61–62, 79–81; leadership, 79–81, 112; nonprofit management study and, 107–108, 135; from nonprofits, 112–113, 135

Life plans, personal, 74–75

Life size contribution, seeing the social sector, 111–115

Listening, importance of, 34–35, 89

Loyalty, workforce and corporate, 10–11

M

Making a Leadership Change (Gilmore), 43

Management programs, nonprofit: college, 107–108; internship, 135

Management qualities and gender, 27–28

Management systems: circular, 53–55, 67–68, 89; hierarchical, 51–52

Manners, and civility, 31–32

Marketing, 89, 108; and the social sector contribution, 111–115

Measurement, performance, 88, 90, 114–115

Metaphors: carrying a big basket, 19–23; the Good Samaritan, 59; putting one's house in order, 72–74

Milestones: eight organization, 66–69; organization viability checklist of, 86–90

Military leaders and personnel, 80, 82, 127

Mission statements: Drucker Foundation, 101; examples of, 14–15, 55–56, 67, 82–83, 101

Mission, the: of changing lives, 111, 114, 137; as essential and enduring, 95–96, 99, 136–137; focus on, 9, 22–23, 86, 106; managing for, 55–56, 60–61; organization-wide knowledge of, 86; questions and issues, 67, 72, 81–82; revisiting the, 66–67, 72, 81–82, 86